" See him [...]
Kept from se[...]
sleuth, on the you[...]ing
— John Piper

WHATEVER HAPPENED TO

TRUTH

The Calvinist

To the mom with an
undying desire for truth
and wisdom, thank you
for your steadfast many
years of friendship.
    Your brother

— Andrew P. Espiny

R. ALBERT MOHLER, JR

J.P. MORELAND

KEVIN J. VANHOOZER

ANDREAS KÖSTENBERGER

WHATEVER HAPPENED TO TRUTH

Andreas Köstenberger

CROSSWAY BOOKS

A PUBLISHING MINISTRY OF
GOOD NEWS PUBLISHERS
WHEATON, ILLINOIS

Published by Crossway Books
    A publishing ministry of Good News Publishers
    1300 Crescent Street
    Wheaton, Illinois 60187

Cover design: Josh Dennis

First printing, 2005

Printed in the United States of America

Library of Congress Cataloging-in-Publication Data
Whatever happened to truth? : / Andreas J. Köstenberger, general editor.
    p. cm.
    Includes bibliographical references and indexes.
    ISBN 1-58134-772-3 (tpb)
    1. Truth—Religious aspects—Christianity. 2. Truth—Biblical teaching.
I. Köstenberger, Andreas J., 1957–
BT50.W35   2005
230.01—dc22   2005027101

CH		15	14	13	12	11	10	09	08	07	06	05
15	14	13	12	11	10	9	8	7	6	5	4	3	2	1

To the One
who is
the Truth,
the Way,
and the Life

"Lord, to whom shall we go?
You have the words of eternal life."
—John 6:68

CONTENTS

INTRODUCTION

Andreas J. Köstenberger

Truth is not what it used to be. In days past, telling the truth meant to represent the facts accurately. It was presupposed that truth corresponded to a reality to be known, and that not telling the truth was morally wrong. To tell a lie, then, was a misrepresentation of a given matter. When former President Bill Clinton claimed, "There is no relationship," in reference to his adulterous affair with a White House intern, was he telling the truth? The well-known response, of course, is that it depends on what the definition of "is" is, as well as on Mr. Clinton's definition of "relationship." Our world has gotten accustomed to Orwellian doublespeak, and with moral absolutes largely considered a thing of the past, language has become a pliable tool in the hands of ideologues.

Feminists have long understood the power of naming and renaming in order to reimagine our world in keeping with their notion of gender equality. But what is considerably more troubling than the tendentious, manipulative use of language by those pursuing sociopolitical agendas is the fact that the very notion of truth has largely become a casualty of postmodern thought and discourse. Truth is no longer "the" truth, in Jesus' terms who claimed to be "the truth" (John 14:6). Rather, it is conceived of as "your" truth or "my" truth—that is, differing yet equally legitimate ways of perceiving reality. Hence truth is simply one's preferred, culturally conditioned, socially constructed version of reality.

Whatever happened to truth?[1] A generation ago Francis Schaeffer coined the phrase "true truth," not in distinction from "false truth," but in recognition of the fact that the very notion of "truth" was under siege already in his day.[2] According to Schaeffer, Christians were to emphatically affirm the possibility and reality of truth by claiming to know "true truth," not merely subjective, relative "truth." As Schaeffer lamented, for modern man, "truth as truth is gone, and . . . relativism reigns."[3] And Schaeffer understood that once truth is torn down in our institutions of higher learning, it is only a matter of time before this will trickle down into our everyday lives.[4]

In his final work, *The Great Evangelical Disaster*, writing in 1984, Schaeffer urged, "Where is the clear voice speaking to the critical issues of the day with distinctively biblical, Christian answers? With tears we must say . . . a large segment of the evangelical world has become seduced by the world . . . we can expect the future to be a further disaster if the evangelical world does not take a stand for biblical truth and morality in the full spectrum of life."[5] Schaeffer's clarion call must be heeded.[6] And yet, it is not sufficient merely to repeat Schaeffer's arguments; a new generation must rise to the challenge of making a case for truth.[7]

In the present work, Albert Mohler, J. P. Moreland, Kevin Vanhoozer, and I join forces to address the issue of truth from a cultural, philosophical, hermeneutical-theological, and biblical perspective respectively. While these essays (first presented as plenary addresses at the 56th Annual Meeting of the Evangelical Theological Society) represent a diversity of viewpoints, which at least in part is a function of the authors' different areas of expertise, they are all written from an evangelical, inerrantist perspective and in the conviction that *there is truth*, and that *truth can be known*, in God's *written* word, the Bible, and in God's *incarnate* Word, the Lord Jesus Christ.

The first essay, "'What Is Truth?' Pilate's Question in Its Johannine and Larger Biblical Context," takes up Pilate's well-known question to Jesus on the nature of truth in John 18:38. It is shown that for John, truth is a theological and, in fact, Christological concept that is inextricably tied to the person of Jesus Christ (John 14:6). God is truth, and his Word is truth (John 17:17), and since Jesus is the Word-become-flesh, the One-of-a-kind Son from the Father, the only way for us to know the truth is to know God through Jesus Christ (John 8:31; 14:6; 17:3).

A defense of the historicity of John's account of Jesus' trial before Pilate and a discussion of this account in light of major Johannine themes is followed by a discussion of the three major characters in Jesus' trial before Pilate: the Jewish leaders, Pilate, and Jesus. The Jewish leaders are shown to bear primary responsibility for Jesus' crucifixion owing to their rejection of truth; Pilate is found to be a perennial reminder of the impossibility of maintaining neutrality in the face of truth; and Jesus, despite the crucifixion, "has in fact not yielded anything, has ultimately lost nothing, and gained everything" as he served as a witness to God's truth before his Roman interrogator.

The study of Jesus' trial before Pilate issues in six important observations concerning truth:

(1) Pilate's question, "What is truth?" masks thick irony, indicating that Jesus' trial before Pilate represented a travesty of justice. If the judge cares nothing about the truth, what does that say about the role of truth in Jesus' trial and the verdict against him?

(2) Pilate's role in fact paralleled that of the Jewish high priest, Caiaphas, so that Jews and Gentiles are shown to unite in an unholy alliance against the Lord's true Anointed.

(3) Truth is not primarily an abstract notion or set of propositions but, Christologically and salvation-historically, inextri-

cably tied to the cross (quite literally so). The truth is Jesus *himself*, and the gospel is about his crucifixion and resurrection. This gospel is what people are called to believe, not some detached statement about reality in general.

(4) The Jewish leaders and Jesus, not Pilate, are the major characters in the trial narrative. Jesus' escalating series of signs in John 1—12 is paralleled by the corresponding groundswell of rejection of Jesus by the Jewish leaders representing the Jewish nation. The major battle for truth is between Jesus and the Jewish leaders and concerns the all-important question of whether or not Jesus is the Messiah he claims to be. While Pilate seeks to *evade* the question of truth, the Jews *reject* the truth outright.

(5) Pilate's question, "What is truth?" far from constituting a sincere inquiry as to the nature of truth, had the mere function of cutting off discussion in order to get on with the business at hand.

(6) Jesus' standing before Pilate pitted truth against power, and in the end the latter was no match for the former. The "power of truth" is infinitely greater than the "truth of power." Hence Jesus gives hope to those who are powerless but who represent the truth.

The essay concludes with a penetrating story told by Václav Havel, writer and long-time dissident and later president of the Czech Republic, that takes its inspiration from the portrayal of truth in John's Gospel.

Albert Mohler's "What Is Truth? Truth and Contemporary Culture" represents a wide-ranging, far-reaching assessment of the state of truth in our postmodern public discourse. As Mohler points out, recent debates over issues such as embryonic stem cell research, human cloning, and same-sex marriage are ultimately arguments about the nature of truth itself, and jurists increasingly view truth not as a matter to be decided but rather to be discovered. However, Mohler observes that postmodernism confronts Christians with a unique set of challenges.

(1) The *deconstruction of truth* means that truth is no longer considered to be universal in scope, but rather relative and subjective. Truth is not absolute or objectively real, but rather socially constructed, a mere human convention subject to change.

(2) The *death of the meta-narrative* ensues in the notion that all comprehensive accounts of truth, meaning, and existence, equally binding for everyone, are cast aside. Not only is all politics local, but all truth is local too. Thus truth is localized. Truth in Los Angeles is different from truth in New Orleans. Truth has no global reach or validity.

(3) The *demise of the text*, including the text of Scripture, follows. If all truth is local, and all meaning is subjective, no text can claim absolute authority or command universal acceptance. Hermeneutics dissolves into cynicism toward the powerful who use texts to control and manipulate others.

(4) Another result of the demise of the notion of absolute truth is what Mohler calls "the *dominion of therapy*." Once the notion of objective, absolute truth has been abandoned, all that remains is fulfilling the desire to be as comfortable as possible. In fact, even theology is reduced to therapy (reminiscent of Paul's reference to people wanting to have "their ears tickled," 2 Tim. 4:3, NASB).

(5) There is a commensurate *decline in authority*, not merely of biblical authority, but of any authority and the notion of authority itself.

(6) The final result is the *displacement of morality*. If there is no absolute truth, there is no firm basis for morality, and prevailing notions of morality become nothing but a person's or group's oppressive exercise of his or her personal beliefs to dominate others.

In the reminder of Mohler's essay, he follows up on this penetrating analysis of postmodern culture, hermeneutics, and morality with an equally compelling call for evangelicals to hold fast to a robust understanding of biblical truth, or else "Christ will not in fact be glorified, the Bible will not be obeyed, the gospel will not be preached, and the Kingdom will not be extended."

In the third major essay, J. P. Moreland, Professor of Philosophy of Religion at Biola University, discusses "Truth, Contemporary Philosophy, and the Postmodern Turn." Moreland contends that postmodernism is "an immoral and cowardly viewpoint" that those who love truth should endeavor to heal. Over against those who would replace the classic correspondence theory of truth—the notion that truth corresponds to reality—with a neo-pragmatic or non-realist model, Moreland identifies himself at the very outset as "an unrepentant correspondence advocate who eschews the various anti-realist views of truth."

Moreland's essay is given to a no-holds-barred, frontal assault on postmodernism and its relativistic understanding of knowledge and truth. According to postmodernism, truth is nothing but the linguistic expression of a socially constructed notion of customs and values characterizing a particular community. Yet, as Moreland contends, postmodernism is plagued by at least five types of confusion:

(1) The notion that truth is a product of Cartesian anxiety, created out of fear of what would result if there were no absolute truth.

(2) A confusion of psychological and rational objectivity: the latter is possible even if the former is not.

(3) An improper disallowance of modest foundationalism—that is, the notion that a proper belief structure is foundational, consisting of properly basic beliefs.

(4) Confusion about truth being found on the sentence level while it is in fact embedded in pre-linguistic structures.

(5) Confusions about perception and intentionality, particularly a rejection of a critical realistic understanding that holds that direct perception is possible.

In the end, Moreland unmasks postmodernism as "a form of intellectual pacifism that, at the end of the day, recommends backgammon while the barbarians are at the gate." It is "the cure that kills the patient, the military strategy that concedes defeat before the first shot is fired, the ideology that undermines its own claims to allegiance."

Following the biblical investigation, cultural analysis, and philosophical critique of postmodernism in the first three essays is Kevin Vanhoozer's creative and brilliant treatise, "Lost in Interpretation? Truth, Scripture, and Hermeneutics." According to Vanhoozer, much recent biblical interpretation has suffered the loss of the author, the interpreter, the subject matter, and, ultimately, the truth. There are four major hermeneutical options (only the last of which is satisfactory): (1) hermeneutical relativism; (2) taking the road to Rome into the bosom of the Roman Catholic Church; (3) joining an independent church; and (4) like Bunyan's Pilgrim, becoming pilgrims on the way, armed with humility, illumined by the Spirit, and in the company of fellow pilgrims following the text.

In discussing the relationship between biblical interpretation and doctrinal truth, Vanhoozer first considers the Hodge-Henry hypothesis, which views doctrine as the result of biblical induction and deduction. In this propositionalist approach to theology, revelation is seen as conveying information that must be processed in order to distill a set of propositional statements. Yet, Vanhoozer contends, this method is inadequate for interpreting textual meaning, because textual meaning cannot be reduced to a set of propositions. According to Vanhoozer, inerrancy by itself does not amount to a full-fledged hermeneutic. A given interpreter's stated belief in inerrancy does not necessarily guarantee an accurate or valid interpretation (though, one might add, neither does the *lack* of an inerrantist position!).

Vanhoozer proceeds to present his own proposal for dealing with the question, What kind of truth does Scripture have, and how does it speak truth? First, he reiterates his opposition to a propositionalist approach that "reduce[s] the truth of Scripture to a set of propositions." We must beware of making the mistake of unduly emphasizing the *content* of Scripture at the expense of its *form*. What gets lost in such a "cheap inerrancy," propositionalist approach is the circumstances underlying a given text as well as its poetic and affective aspects and hence a dimension of the truth conveyed by it.

Second, Vanhoozer sets forth what he considers to be a better way for understanding scriptural truth. He contends that biblical interpretation must begin with an appreciation of the fact that *truth is expressed in the interface between an author's discourse (interpreted in context) and the way things are.* What, then, is the primary subject matter of scriptural truth? Vanhoozer's answer is, "the creative and redemptive work of the triune God," to be understood in the context of a true catholicity that serves as an antidote to interpretive tribalism and parochialism.

According to Vanhoozer, the Bible sets forth *theodrama*— the words and acts of God in the course of history climaxing in Jesus Christ, and truth is to be conceived as *theodramatic correspondence.* Scripture is the *script* to this theodrama, and we are all *participants* receiving "performance knowledge" and doctrinal direction. "Truth is the fit between text and reality," and the task of interpretation is to learn to read the map of the biblical text in its various genres and literary forms of expression.

Finally, what about the process of finding truth in and through interpretation? First, we must rightly assess the *historical* dimension of Scripture. History is so tightly wedded to biblical literature and narrative that the two cannot truly be separated. Second, we must move beyond understanding *words* to understanding *discourse*; "hermeneutics is the art of discerning the discourse in written works." This, third, must take place within the context of an appreciation of the importance of literary *genres* for proper interpretation. As Vanhoozer contends, "the *literal* [not literalistic] sense is the *literary* sense."[8]

"The literal sense of Scripture as a whole," in turn, "is the theodramatic sense." Discerning this theodramatic sense, says Vanhoozer, requires imagination, "the power of synoptic vision": "the purpose of exegesis is not to excavate but to explore canonically-embodied truth by becoming apprentices to the literary forms, and this involves more than mastering the propositional content. By learning imaginatively to follow and indwell the biblical texts, we see through them to reality as it really is 'in Christ.'"

Enjoy, then, fellow pilgrim, the trek from exploring the meaning of Pilate's question to Jesus, "What is truth?" to engaging in analysis of twenty-first-century culture to navigating the labyrinth of postmodern confusion to venturing on the arduous yet rewarding path toward accurate "literal" biblical interpretation. Let's debrief together at the end of our journey for some moments of recommissioning and farewell.

Andreas J. Köstenberger
Wake Forest, NC
September 11, 2005

1

"WHAT IS TRUTH?"
PILATE'S QUESTION IN ITS
JOHANNINE AND LARGER
BIBLICAL CONTEXT

Andreas J. Köstenberger

*Andreas J. Köstenberger, professor of New Testament at Southeastern
Baptist Theological Seminary, Wake Forest, North Carolina, and editor
of the Journal of the Evangelical Theological Society, delivered this plenary address at the 56th annual meeting of the Evangelical Theological
Society on November 17, 2004, in San Antonio, Texas.*

"What is truth?"[1] It is hard to imagine a more profound
question with more momentous consequences. A quest
for truth has driven the world's greatest philosophers and theologians. "What is truth?" is also the question Pilate asked Jesus
according to John. Has Pilate therefore gone among the philosophers? Few are prepared to argue this. More likely, Pilate's question has several layers of meaning, which is why it has intrigued
commentators over the centuries and continues to exercise a fas-
cination that pays tribute not so much to the one who originally
asked the question but to the evangelist and theologian who

wove the question into the fabric of his Gospel concerning Jesus, the Christ and Son of God.

In the following essay I will take a fresh look at the ramifications of Pilate's question, "What is truth?" in John 18:38[2] in the immediate context of John's account of Jesus' Roman trial (18:28—19:16a) and the larger context of the Johannine passion narrative (18—19) and the farewell discourse (13—17) and ultimately the entire Gospel.[3] After a few introductory remarks on the concept of truth, I will, first, assess the historicity of 18:33-38a; second, probe the relationship between the passage and major themes in John's Gospel; and, third, look at the three major characters in 18:28—19:16a. I will close with several observations concerning John's account of Jesus' trial before Pilate, related to Pilate's question to Jesus, "What is truth?"

I. WHAT IS TRUTH?

The term "truth" had currency in Greek philosophy, Roman thought, and the Hebrew Bible (including its many uses in the LXX).[4] In Greek philosophy, one of the senses of *alētheia* involved an accurate perspective on reality.[5] Romans similarly spoke of *veritas* as a factual representation of events.[6] In the Hebrew Scriptures, "truth" (*'emeth*, *'emunah*) primarily conveyed the notion of God's faithfulness.[7] This faithfulness had been revealed throughout the history of Israel and, according to John, found supreme expression in the life, ministry, and substitutionary death of Jesus (1:14; 14:6).[8]

In John's Gospel, where the importance of "truth" is underscored by forty-eight instances of the *aleth*-word group in comparison with a combined total of ten in the Synoptics,[9] the notion of truth is inextricably related to God, and to Jesus' relationship with God.[10] Is Jesus the Son of God, or is he guilty of blasphemy (cf. esp. Matt. 26:59-66; Mark 14:55-64; Luke 22:66-71)?[11] Jesus claims he is the Son of God, and the fourth evangelist's purpose for writing his Gospel is tied up with demonstrating the veracity of Jesus' claim (20:30-31). The Jewish leaders, on the other hand, consider Jesus a blasphemer (5:18; 8:59; 10:33-36; 19:7).

In John, then, truth is first and foremost a theological, and perhaps even more accurately, a Christological concept.[12] Rather than merely connoting correspondence with reality, as in Greek philosophy, or factual accuracy, as in Roman thought, truth, for John, while also being propositional, is at the heart a personal, relational concept that has its roots and origin in none other than God himself. As the psalmist (Ps. 31:5, NIV) and the prophet (Isa. 65:16) call God "the God of truth," so John's Gospel proclaims that God is truth, and that therefore his Word is truth.[13] Jesus, then, is the truth, because he is sent from God and has come to reveal the Father and to carry out his salvation-historical purposes.[14] For this reason the only way for us to know the truth is to know God through Jesus Christ (8:31; 14:6; 17:3).

II. The Historicity of John's Account of Jesus' Trial Before Pilate

What is the truth about the historicity of John's account of Jesus' trial before Pilate? Did John invent the present passage, as David Friedrich Strauss believed, perhaps, as Ferdinand Baur surmised, to transfer guilt from Pilate to the Jewish leaders, a view recently revived by Maurice Casey, who repeatedly charges John with "rewriting history"?[15] Did John merely imagine Jesus' interchange with Pilate, as James Dunn argues in his recent book *Jesus Remembered*?[16] Is Andrew Lincoln correct in his contention that it is "not plausible to defend any consistent or detailed one-to-one correspondence between John's narrative and what is likely to have happened in the ministry of Jesus"?[17] Or is John's account historically reliable?[18]

In setting the stage, all four Gospels make reference to Jesus being led from Caiaphas to the governor's palace (Matt. 27:1-2; Mark 15:1; Luke 23:1; John 18:28). Only John adds that the Jewish leaders did not enter the palace in order not to defile themselves so that they would be able to eat the Passover, no doubt an instance of Johannine irony. While the Jewish leaders had no scruples about crucifying the one who embodied the very reality to which the Passover pointed, they were scrupulous in their observance of sacrificial law. This historical detail supplied only by John is eminently credible and in keeping with what we know of first-century Judaism.[19]

At this point, Matthew recounts the death of Judas; neither John nor the other Synoptic writers interrupt their account of Jesus' trial before Pilate to do the same. John's Gospel proceeds to narrate the interchange between Pilate and the Jewish leaders when Jesus is handed over to the governor. In John 18:30, the Jewish leaders identify Jesus as "evildoer" (NASB), with no further specifics given at this point (though see later 19:7). Luke specifies beyond this that the Jewish leaders charged Jesus with "perverting our nation, and forbidding us to give tribute to Caesar, and saying that he himself is Christ a king" (Luke 23:2, RSV; cf. Matt. 22:15-22; Mark 12:13-17; Luke 20:19-26). This fills in a narrative gap in John's Gospel, where the Jewish leaders are shown to identify Jesus as an evildoer in 18:30 and Pilate asks Jesus in 18:33 if he is "the king of the Jews," an identification not previously narrated in John's Gospel. As Luke 23:2 shows, the Jewish leaders had in fact charged Jesus with claiming to be "Christ, a king," whereby the latter epithet glosses "Christ" in terms of "a king" originally for the benefit of the Gentile Pilate, and in the case of Luke's Gospel for the benefit of his Gentile readers.

The following question, "Are you the king of the Jews?" is the same word for word in all four Gospels,[20] as is Jesus' later

response, "You have said so."[21] Apart from this, the Johannine
account of Jesus' first interrogation before Pilate in John 18:33-
38a is unique to John's Gospel. Subsequently, Luke records
again the specific charge by the Jewish leaders that Jesus was
"stir[ring] up the people" through his teaching throughout all
Judea including Galilee (Luke 23:5), at which point Pilate
inquired whether Jesus was a Galilean (underscoring Pilate's
ignorance of particulars regarding Jesus). When told that it was
so, Pilate, according to Luke, sent Jesus to Herod Antipas, striking an alliance with the Galilean ruler who had previously been
a foe (Luke 23:6-12).

Like John, all the Synoptics then record the Barabbas incident (Matt. 27:15-23; Mark 15:6-14; Luke 23:17-23; John
18:39-40), with Matthew including also a reference to Pilate's
wife's dream and her warning issued to her husband to have
nothing to do with "that righteous man" (i.e., Jesus; Matt.
27:19). The scourging of Jesus, the crown of thorns, the dark red
robe, the mock homage of Jesus, all recounted in John 19:1-3,
are likewise closely paralleled in the Synoptic Gospels (specifically, Matt. 27:28-31a and Mark 15:17-20a). The following
narrative, John 19:4-15, involving Pilate's further interchange
with the Jewish leaders and with Jesus culminating in the Jewish
leaders' claim that they have no king but Caesar (19:15), is again
unique to John's Gospel.

Overall, it appears that wherever John's Gospel does over-
lap with one or several of the Synoptic Gospels, the Synoptics
corroborate John's account very closely. Clearly, however, once
again John has written his own Gospel, issuing in his inclusion
of the material found in John 18:33-38a and 19:4-15. Nothing
in these verses is historically implausible or otherwise suspect in
terms of its historicity.[22] I believe that John was most likely
aware of the Synoptic accounts of Jesus' passion, whether or not
John had the Synoptics in front of him as he wrote (I personally

doubt that he had).[23] On the basis of those accounts, it is probable that John sought to supplement the information given in the Synoptics, specifically with regard to the nature of Jesus' kingdom. It is intriguing that this topic occupies considerable space especially in Matthew's and Luke's Gospels while it is otherwise virtually ignored in John.[24] Perhaps Jesus' comments regarding the nature of his kingdom to Pilate in John's Gospel serve as a functional substitute for the kingdom parables in the Synoptics. Beyond this, the repeated references to truth and the reference to witness in 18:33-38a tie in closely with the larger "truth" and "witness" themes in John's Gospel.

But how are we to assess the historicity of the two interchanges between Pilate and Jesus that are unique to John's Gospel (18:33-38a and 19:4-15)? One important aspect of this evaluation is bound up with what we know of Pilate's history as governor. The question then becomes, "Is the way Pilate acts in these Johannine passages consistent with what we know of him from other extant sources (including, but not limited to, the Synoptic Gospels)?" Is there evidence for Pilate's antagonism toward the Jews that is displayed in his comment in 18:35, "Am I a Jew?" (see also 18:31). Is there evidence for Pilate's vulnerability to the charge that if he lets Jesus go, he is no friend of Caesar (19:12)? The answer to both questions is an unqualified, "Yes."

Pontius[25] Pilate, governor of Judea,[26] was appointed to his post by the emperor Tiberius in A.D. 26 and held this position for about ten years until A.D. 36/37.[27] Pilate owed his appointment to Lucius Aelius Sejanus, the commander of the praetorian guard in Rome (cf. Philo, Gaius 24 §159).[28] If, as I have argued in my commentary, the date of Jesus' trial and crucifixion is A.D. 33 (rather than A.D. 30), and in light of the fact that Pilate's mentor Sejanus died on October 18, A.D. 31, Pilate would have lost his major supporter with the Roman emperor.[29] This would have

"What Is Truth?" Pilate's Question in Its Johannine and Larger Biblical Context

25

necessitated that Pilate tread more lightly and would have rendered him more vulnerable with his superiors. Especially if Jesus' trial took place in A.D. 33, subsequent to Sejanus's death, Pilate's vulnerability to Jewish intimidation makes eminent historical sense.[30]

As to Pilate's uneasy relationship with the Jews, the Jewish historian Josephus reports several clashes between Pilate and the Jewish population. One such incident involved Pilate's erection of statues of Caesar in Jerusalem. Since this is the first incident mentioned in the account of Pilate in both the Jewish War (2.169-74) and the Antiquities of the Jews (18.55-59), it appears the most likely date for this episode is A.D. 26/27, the first year of Pilate's gubernatorial tenure.[31] In this incident, Pilate had Roman standards with the embossed figures of the emperor set up in Jerusalem by night, to the consternation of the Jews. But Pilate refused all protests and gave orders for his soldiers to draw their swords. Yet when he saw the Jews' resolve and willingness to die for their faith, he relented and had the effigies removed. At another occasion, still prior to Jesus' crucifixion, Pilate did not relent and inflicted a large number of casualties on the Jews (Josephus, *J.W.* 2.175-77; cf. *Ant.* 18.60-62). Luke, likewise, tells of an occasion where some "told Jesus about the Galileans whose blood Pilate had mixed with their sacrifices" (Luke 13:1).[32] These events during Pilate's gubernatorial tenure add up to the picture of a ruthless, violent ruler torn hopelessly between his subjects and his Roman bosses.

The incident that finally led to Pilate's removal from office in A.D. 36, only three years after Jesus' crucifixion, illustrates very well that Pilate's position had gotten considerably more tenuous subsequent to Sejanus's death.

The issue at stake was a Samaritan uprising that had been brutally put down by Pilate. Vitellius, the governor of Syria, ordered Pilate to return to Rome to give the emperor an account of his handling of the uprising, and so, as Josephus tells us, "Pilate, after having spent ten years in Judaea, hurried to Rome in obedience to the orders of Vitellius, since he could not refuse" (*Ant.* 18.88-89).[33] These pieces of evidence from Josephus and Luke strongly support the historicity of John's accounts of Pilate's behavior in 18:28—19:16a, including his animosity toward the Jews and his vulnerability to the charge that if he let Jesus go, this proved that he was no friend of the Roman emperor.

There is yet another important vantage point from which we may assess the historicity of John's account of Jesus' trial before Pilate—namely, how Jesus' pattern of behavior in the two major scenes of interrogation in 18:33-38a and 19:9-11 matches the way he is portrayed elsewhere in this and the other canonical Gospels. Again, as will be seen, on this count as well we come away with a strong indication of authenticity. Specifically, there is, first, the way in which Jesus responds to questions. In the present instance, we find three distinctive ways in which Jesus interacts with Pilate:

> (1) by asking a counter-question (18:34: "Do you say this of your own accord, or did others say it to you about me?");
>
> (2) by providing an indirect answer that reframes the issue in Jesus' rather than the questioner's terms (18:36: "My kingdom is not of this world") or that takes the conversation in a different direction in some other way (18:37, RSV: "You say that I am a king. For this purpose I was born . . ."); and
>
> (3) by remaining silent (19:10; but see 19:11).

To this should be added, fourth, Jesus' characteristic reluctance to speak about his messianic claims and identity, especially without defining his terms, which pervades both interchanges with Pilate (18:33-38a; 19:9).

In each case, Jesus' conduct is amply corroborated by similar patterns both in John's and in the other Gospels. (1) Jesus frequently asks counter-questions rather than answering questions immediately (e.g., Matt. 15:3; 21:24; 22:18-19; Mark 10:3; Luke 10:26). (2) He regularly provides indirect answers (e.g., Matt. 11:4-6; 21:24-27; 22:18-21). In fact, Jesus' very words in John 18:37, "You say that I am . . .," are paralleled in the Synoptic account of Jesus' Jewish trial before Caiaphas (Matt. 26:64; Luke 22:70). (3) The Synoptics repeatedly mention that Jesus remained silent when questioned (Matt. 26:63; 27:14; Mark 14:61; 15:5; Luke 23:9; cf. Isa. 53:7). (4) Jesus' reluctance to speak about his messianic claims and identity is widely known as a characteristic feature of the Synoptic portrait of Jesus and is often identified by the label "the messianic secret."[34]

Finally, Jesus' speaking to Pilate about his "kingdom" provides a strong link with the Synoptics where Jesus' teaching about the kingdom is one of the major (if not the most prominent) motifs (e.g., the kingdom parables found in Matthew 13 and 18).

Beyond this, of course, it is important to remember how John's own claim to be providing accurate eyewitness testimony is inextricably related to the Johannine concept of truth itself, where testimony is an indispensable component of that concept (such that the true God is most fully and finally known through the Son who bears testimony to him, 1:18; the Spirit's role is similar: 15:26). It would therefore be the height of incongruity if a biblical writer who stresses the eyewitness character of his account in keeping with the nature of Jesus' and the Spirit's roles (compare 13:23 with 1:18) were to invent or "imagine" stories that he knows never took place for the sake of teaching a theological lesson about Jesus that lacks an actual historical core.[35]

For these reasons the historicity of John's account of Jesus' trial before Pilate should be regarded as established with a high degree of probability. Both from the vantage point of Pilate's

known political situation and character, and of Jesus' well-cor-
roborated pattern of responding to questions and discussing his
messianic identity, John's portrait is thoroughly compatible with
that of the Synoptics and coherent within itself and with the rest
of the Fourth Gospel.

III. THE ACCOUNT OF JESUS' TRIAL BEFORE PILATE IN LIGHT OF MAJOR JOHANNINE THEMES

John's account of Jesus' trial before Pilate, particularly in John
18:33-38a, forms an integral part of at least three major
Johannine themes: the trial motif, Jesus' kingship, and the theme
of truth. Regarding the first motif, Bultmann speaks of "the
great trial between God and the world" that provides the larger
backdrop for Jesus' Jewish and Roman trials. While Pilate is
Jesus' judge according to the world's standards, the reader
already knows that, in truth, it is Jesus who is the judge who
decides over life and death (5:19-29).[36]

More recently, A. T. Lincoln has argued that the "witness"
and "judgment" word groups are part of a "cosmic trial" or
"lawsuit motif" in John's Gospel "in which Jesus as God's
uniquely authorized agent acts as both witness and judge."[37]
According to Lincoln, the lawsuits between God and the nations
as well as God and Israel in the Septuagint of Isaiah 40—55 form
the background for the Johannine "lawsuit motif." In the context
of the lawsuit, truth stands for the whole process of judging, culminating in the verdict. At the heart of John's Gospel is the question of whether or not the crucified Jesus is the Messiah (20:31)
and whether or not he rightly claimed to be one with God.
"Truth" is in essence an affirmative answer to these questions.
The reason why John does not record a Jewish trial is because
Jesus' entire ministry is conceived in terms of a trial (1—12).

The second major Johannine theme found in the present
passage is that of Jesus' kingship. At the very outset of John's

Gospel, Jesus is acknowledged as the "King of Israel" by Nathanael (1:49), though it is possible that Nathanael's understanding of the entailments of this term carried nationalistic overtones.[38] Misunderstanding is even more evident in people's effort to make Jesus their king subsequent to the feeding of the multitude in John 6 (see esp. 6:14). While the references to Jesus as the "king of Israel" at the triumphal entry into Jerusalem in 12:13, 15 appear to be more positive, the context there reveals that, once again, people do not truly understand the nature of Jesus' kingship. In fact, the same crowds who acclaim Jesus at that occasion less than a week later join the Jewish leaders in calling for Jesus' crucifixion.

In contrast to "king of Israel," which is essentially a positive reference, the expression "King of the Jews," as used by Pilate, seems to be somewhat derogatory (18:33, 39; 19:3, 19, 21 [*bis*]; cf. 19:14, 15: "your King").[39] This may be one reason why Jesus does not directly affirm being this figure when asked by Pilate, not once, but twice, whether or not he is the "King of the Jews" (18:33, 37). While Jesus is therefore reluctant to identify himself as king (cf. 6:14)—though he does enter Jerusalem on his final visit to the city in messianic fashion (12:13, 15)—he speaks openly about his kingdom (18:36). Even so, the only thing Jesus says about his kingdom is what it is not:[40] it is not of this world.[41] This provides Pilate with the information he needs to assess the merits of the Jewish charges against Jesus as a potential threat to Roman imperial power: Jesus' denial—as well as presumably his harmless personal demeanor and appearance—is sufficient for Pilate to determine that, whatever religious motives the Jewish leaders may have had in incriminating Jesus, on political grounds he poses no threat to Rome. Beyond this, Pilate is not interested in the purpose of Jesus' mission, which in the present passage is circumscribed as witnessing to the truth (18:37).

Truth, in conjunction with witness, is a third major motif found in John's Gospel.[42] While truth and witness are part of the larger Johannine trial theme, it will be helpful to look at "truth" terminology in the Gospel in its own right as it unfolds in the narrative.[43] The first two relevant references to truth, *alētheia*, are found in the prologue, where the evangelist writes that Jesus is full of grace and truth (1:14) and that grace and truth came through Jesus Christ (1:17).

In light of the numerous parallels between 1:14-17 and Exodus 33—34, it is highly likely that the phrase "grace and truth" (*charis kai alētheia*) in John's prologue harks back to the phrase "steadfast love and faithfulness" (*hesed ve'emeth*) in Exodus 34:6.[44] While Moses was unable to see God (Exod. 33:20-23), the one-of-a-kind Son of the Father has made him known (John 1:18); and while Moses was the mediator of the law (Exod. 34), the fullness of God's grace and truth came through Jesus Christ (John 1:17).[45] The subsequent Gospel proceeds to explicate and substantiate this claim.[46]

Tracing the instances of "truth" in the Gospel sequentially, and referring the reader to my commentary on John for a more detailed treatment of individual passages, we read in 4:23-24 that worship of God must be rendered in spirit and truth (perhaps harking back to the phrase "in sincerity and truth" in Josh. 24:14, NASB)[47] and that John the Baptist came as a witness to the truth (5:33, a passage that parallels and anticipates Jesus' self-reference in 18:37).[48] The climactic (seven) references to truth in the first half of John's Gospel occur in chapter 8, where Jesus exhorts those who had "believed in him" to continue in his teaching, so that they may know the truth, which will set them free (implying that his teaching is truth; 8:32).[49] In 8:40, Jesus identifies himself as "a man who has told you the truth" (cf. Jer. 9:5; Zech. 8:16; and esp. 2 Chron. 18:15; see also John 8:45-46), in contrast to the devil, who

does not stand in the truth, and in whom there is no truth
(8:44; cf. Gen. 3:4-5).[50]

The next set of references is found in the farewell discourse. Importantly, truth takes on a trinitarian dimension[51]
when, in 14:6, *Jesus* is identified as the way, the truth, and the
life (cf. 1:14, 17; see also 1QH 4:40: "for you [O God] are
truth");[52] the *Holy Spirit* is called "the Spirit of truth" in
14:17; 15:26; and 16:13 (cf. 1 John 4:6; 5:6; 1QS 3:18-19;
4:23), who will guide believers in all truth (16:13; cf. Ps. 25:5);
and God's (the *Father's*) Word is described as truth (17:17; cf.
Ps. 119:160; Jer. 10:10; see also 2 Sam. 7:28; 1 Kings 17:24;
Ps. 119:142, 151), in which believers are to be consecrated
(17:19; cf. 1QS 4:20-21).[53]

John 17:17-19 is also the major passage other than 18:37
where "truth" and "world" are juxtaposed. The term *kosmos*
occurs as many as eight times in the span of 17:14-19, and
alētheia is found three times in 17:17-19. This suggests that John
envisions Jesus' appearance before Pilate as a paradigmatic
instance of one who was not of the world but who was set apart
and sent into the world to speak the truth, which is God's word.
Jesus' witness to the truth served as a model for his followers to
emulate (cf. 17:18; 20:21).

These references to "truth" in John's Gospel set the stage for
Jesus' interchange with Pilate in 18:37-38, which includes the
final three references to truth in John's Gospel. The instances of
alētheia in 18:37-38, then, provide some closure to the presentation of truth in the Johannine narrative. Jesus' mission is
summed up as bearing witness to the truth (cf. 3:11, 32; 7:7;
8:14);[54] everyone who is of the truth listens to Jesus; and Pilate
is dismissive of, or at least indifferent to, the truth. Quite likely,
the three references to truth in 18:36-38 constitute an inclusio
with the three references to grace and truth in 1:14-17.

If so, rather than repeating the allusion to God's covenant

faithfulness struck in the prologue, the present passage indicates progression in that, according to the fourth evangelist, truth now has come before Pilate, the Roman, Gentile governor, which is in keeping with the universal message of the Gospel. As in Luke-Acts, there is therefore a movement from Jew to Gentile.[55] In the context of the entire Johannine narrative, similar to the ending of Luke-Acts, Pilate's question, "What is truth?" remains open-ended, and still rings through the ages, calling for an answer from every reader of the Gospel.[56]

IV. THE MAJOR CHARACTERS IN JESUS' TRIAL BEFORE PILATE

While it may appear that the two major characters in the present passage are Jesus and Pilate, a third group of people looms large in the background: the Jewish leaders. It is they who charged Jesus with sedition, and it is they whom Pilate is trying to appease in the way he deals with Jesus. For this reason, a literary investigation of Pilate's trial before Jesus must properly commence with a study of the Jewish leaders.[57]

1. *The Jewish leaders.* The Jewish leaders' hostility toward Jesus grows steadily in John's Gospel, particularly during the second half of Jesus' public ministry narrated in John 5—12. The entire first half of John's Gospel narrates a total of seven signs, directed specifically toward the Jewish people to convince them that Jesus is in fact the long-expected Messiah.[58] Jesus had turned water into wine at the Cana wedding (2:1-12), had cleared the Jerusalem Temple in a startling display of his messianic authority (2:14-22), had healed the centurion's son long-distance (4:45-54), healed the lame man (5:1-15), fed the multitudes (6:1-15), opened the eyes of the man born blind (chap. 9), and raised Lazarus from the dead (chap. 11). Yet at the end of this long string of striking displays of Jesus' messianic identity, the Jewish leaders were more hardened toward Jesus'

"What Is Truth?" Pilate's Question in Its Johannine and Larger Biblical Context

33

claims than ever before and ever more determined to kill the one who claimed to be the Son of God but whom they considered to be a mere messianic pretender, deceiver, and blasphemer.

The evangelist's closing indictment of the Jewish nation as represented by its leaders is therefore severe: "Though he [Jesus] had done so many signs before them, they still did not believe in him" (12:37). As the evangelist proceeds to note, however, in God's sovereign providence, the Jewish leaders' hardening toward God's salvific purposes in and through Jesus fulfilled Scripture, particularly Isaiah's words in Isaiah 53:1 and 6:10 (John 12:38, 40). What is more, as the evangelist makes clear, by its rejection of Jesus as Messiah, the Jewish nation joined the world at large in its sinful rejection of the truth.

The second major unit of John's Gospel (13—21) is consequently devoted to the Messiah's formation and instruction of a new messianic community made up of those who believed in him. While every single member of the Twelve, Jesus' inner circle, was Jewish, it was not their Jewishness that commended these followers but their faith in Jesus as Messiah. What is already implicit in the evangelist's closing verdict in chapter 12 plays itself out in the passion narrative in chapters 18—19 where the Jewish leaders intimidate the Roman procurator to accede to their wishes and to give his consent to have Jesus crucified.

In his narration of Jesus' passion, the fourth evangelist seems to presuppose the Synoptic passion narratives. He does not cover Jesus' formal Sanhedrin trial before Caiaphas (skipping over it in 18:24, 28), which is narrated in some detail in the Synoptics. At the same time, he recounts Jesus' interrogation by Pilate in considerably more detail. Why this shift in perspective? It is hard to be certain, but it is possible that the evangelist believes he has already demonstrated the hardening of the Jewish leaders in the first half of his Gospel, culminating in

Caiaphas's statement in 11:49-50 and in the negative verdict of 12:37, so that he focuses his trial narrative on Pilate's complicity in the world's rejection of the Messiah, which, as mentioned above, also includes Jesus' rejection by his own people, the Jews.

In lodging charges against Jesus, the Jewish leaders display a shrewd yet deceptive progression from presenting Jesus to the Roman governor initially as a common criminal (18:30).[59] Only later, when Pilate appears inclined to free Jesus, do they reveal the real reason why they wanted Jesus dead: "We have a law, and according to that law he ought to die because he has made himself the Son of God" (19:7). A second tactic employed by the Jewish leaders is that of manipulation and intimidation. When their lobbying for Jesus' death seems to fall on deaf ears, they tell Pilate, "If you release this man, you are not Caesar's friend. Everyone who makes himself a king opposes Caesar" (19:12). Here they frame in political terms—Jesus' kingship—what they in fact perceived as a religious claim, Jesus' divine sonship, fully aware that this rendered Pilate vulnerable to his Roman superiors. In the end, the Jewish leaders prevail and get their wish when Pilate delivers Jesus over to be crucified (19:16)—but not before disavowing their own messianic hopes and professing before Pilate to "have no king but Caesar" (19:15) in a massive betrayal of their own religious heritage (cf. Judg. 8:23; 1 Sam. 8:7; Isa. 26:13 where God is said to be Israel's only king).[60]

Hence, according to the fourth evangelist, the Jewish leaders are the driving force behind the crucifixion of Jesus. On one level, the Jewish authorities emerge as the temporary victors from the present incident. They get their way, and Jesus is handed over to them by Pilate to be crucified. Yet their victory is Pyrrhic on several counts. First, in order to gain Pilate's concession, they pledge sole allegiance to the Roman emperor (19:15). Thus Pilate's cooperation is secured at a very high cost. Second, prevailing upon Pilate to condemn Jesus to die implicates the Jews in crucifying not only an innocent man, but the God-sent Messiah. By this they incur great guilt (cf. Matt. 27:25) and unwittingly collaborate with Satan in opposing the purposes of God.[61]

In contrast to Pilate, who, as will be seen, lacks spiritual insight to comprehend the true nature of the Jewish case against Jesus and the spiritual dimension of his kingdom, the Jewish leaders are fully aware of the import of Jesus' claim of being the Messiah.[62] While Pilate thus is part of the Johannine "misunderstanding" theme (witness Pilate's repeated ignorant references to Jesus as "the king of the Jews"), the Jewish leaders are shown to reject Jesus in the full knowledge of his actions (the "signs") and affirmations of oneness with God (e.g., 10:30). By his characterization of the Jewish leaders, not only in the present passage but throughout his Gospel, John places the primary responsibility for Jesus' crucifixion squarely on them.

2. Pilate. In his dealings with the Jewish leaders, Pilate displays the customary reluctance of Roman government officials to get involved in what he perceives to be inner-Jewish religious affairs (e.g., Gallio; Acts 18:14-15). However, in the ensuing interrogation, nothing seems to go as Pilate has planned, and things increasingly spin out of control.[63] Pilate's first attempt to extricate himself from the situation has him tell the Jewish leaders, "Take him yourselves and judge him by your own law" (18:31).[64] Yet because only the Romans had jurisdiction to put a man to death, and because it was death that the Jewish leaders wanted for Jesus, Pilate's first attempt to avoid dealing with Jesus, coupled with the Jewish leaders' resolve to have Jesus crucified, fails.

This is followed by Pilate's first of two private interrogations of Jesus narrated in John's Gospel, culminating in Pilate's question, "What is truth?" (18:33-38).[65] The narrative does not explain why Pilate, having been told that Jesus was an evildoer

(18:30), asks Jesus whether or not he is "the King of the Jews" (18:33). The answer is, however, intimated in Jesus' counter-question in 18:34, "Do you say this of your own accord, or did others say it to you about me?" Very likely, the Jewish leaders had implicated Jesus as a political threat to Roman imperial rule in Palestine, and it is this charge that Pilate sets out to investigate.[66]

Pilate's answer to Jesus reveals both a possible anti-Semitic streak ("Am I a Jew?," 18:35)[67] and a hint of impatience: "Your own nation and the chief priests have delivered you over to me. What have you done?" (18:35, *Ti epoiēsas;* echoing *kakon poiōn* in 18:30; see also Matt. 27:23: "What evil has he done?").[68] Beyond this, Pilate may also be offended at what he may consider Jesus' insinuation that he is merely parroting the charge leveled against him by the Jewish leaders. If so, Pilate here asserts his own independent judgment. He is not a puppet but is conducting his own investigation. Ironically, however, Pilate's verdict does not reflect his own independent judgment (i.e., that Jesus is innocent) but falls in line with the verdict already reached by the Jewish leaders. Hence Jesus' insinuation proves correct: this is not a true fact-finding mission but a hasty affair in which truth is not served.

Pilate's interaction with Jesus also reveals that he does not know much (if anything) about Jesus and his claims and actions as they have been narrated in the first half of the Gospel (cf. Luke 23:5-7). Clearly, his assumption is that Jesus must have done something to draw the intense hatred and opposition of the Jewish leaders, and he expects him to confess what it is he has done to attract such antagonism.

Jesus' answer, however, does nothing of the sort. Rather than confess his wrong, Jesus corrects the impression Pilate has been given by the Jewish leaders regarding the nature of Jesus' kingship. Jesus' kingdom is not of this world. Jesus indeed has a kingdom, and he is indeed a king, but his kingdom and kingship are tied up, not with political exploits, but with truth. And it is to this truth that Jesus has come to witness. As Pilate's question, "What is truth?" makes clear (a rhetorical question that expects no answer),[69] he is not the least interested in this kind of kingdom.[70] Pilate did not even want to take up Jesus' case to begin with; he is even less interested in listening to Jesus' elaboration on the nature of his kingdom or on the more precise substance of the truth to which he came to witness.[71] If Jesus does not present a political threat, he ought to be released. In what follows, Pilate never wavers from his conviction that Jesus ought to be released and caves in only to persistent Jewish demands to have him executed (18:38b—19:16a).

In some sense, then, similar to the Jewish leaders, Pilate seems to come out on top of both of the other protagonists, Jesus and the Jewish leaders.[72] Pilate does not give in to the Jews' demands until they have pledged allegiance to Rome, and Jesus is removed as a potential threat to Roman authority in Palestine. Yet, as Alan Culpepper points out, Pilate's, too, is a hollow victory. In fact, it is no victory at all. All of his actions serve the purpose of avoiding to make a decision regarding Jesus. In the end, this strategy failed; the Jewish leaders forced Pilate's hand, and he made his decision—against Jesus. Again, Culpepper is correct in noting that everything that follows— the inscription on the cross, the permission to hasten death by having Jesus' legs broken, and the approval of a proper burial—constitutes attempts by Pilate to atone for condemning a man to die who he sensed was innocent. Culpepper's conclusion regarding Pilate is worth quoting in full:

> Like other characters caught between the Jews and Jesus (principally Nicodemus, the lame man, and the blind man), Pilate is a study in the impossibility of compromise, the inevitability of

decision, and the consequences of each alternative. In the end, although he seems to glimpse the truth, a decision in Jesus' favor proves too costly for him. In this maneuver to force the reader to a decision regarding Jesus, the evangelist exposes the consequences of attempting to avoid a decision. Pilate represents the futility of attempted compromise. The reader who tries to temporize or escape through the gate of indecision will find Pilate as his companion along that path.[73]

The parallelism with Nicodemus is particularly evident.[74] Nicodemus, the Jewish rabbi, does not understand the entrance requirement into the kingdom of God—spiritual regeneration. Pilate, the Roman governor, does not comprehend the nature of Jesus' kingdom—truth. In both cases, their conversation with Jesus ends on an abrupt note with an exasperated question on their part. "How can these things be?" Nicodemus asks, revealing his lack of understanding of spiritual realities. "What is truth?" is Pilate's question, displaying his lack of understanding of the true truth that can be comprehended only by those who first embrace the Truth sent from God and are guided by the Spirit of truth.[75]

In the end, therefore, Pilate is a tragic figure who fails to realize the momentous significance of the present encounter. His curt dismissal of the larger question of truth will have eternal personal consequences, and he can ill afford to brush aside the issue as glibly as he does. In fact, through Pilate, the evangelist teaches us something quite profound about the connection between Jesus and truth, namely, that the more one knows who Jesus is (who is the truth), the more one must become apathetic about the issue of truth itself if one is to continue rejecting Jesus.[76] In contrast to Jesus' great humility (evidenced, among other things, by his mere self-reference as a "witness to the truth"), Pilate displays considerable arrogance in the way he deals with the one charged with wrongdoing who stands before

him. In this, Pilate serves as a representative character of all
those who fail to recognize that they are called to render a verdict regarding Jesus and who deem themselves to be in the judgment seat regarding Jesus while in fact it is they who will be
judged on the basis of their decision concerning Jesus.

In an act that has profound supernatural consequences,
Pilate, in Bultmann's words, "shuts the door on the claim of the
revelation, and in so doing he shows that he is not of the truth—
he is of the lie."[77] But, as Bultmann points out, Pilate is different from the Jewish leaders who are bent on killing Jesus and on
perpetrating a lie in keeping with the intentions of their true spiritual father, the devil (8:44). Pilate is not a Jew, so that for him
it is not envy (Matt. 27:18; Mark 15:10) or religious prejudice
that might cause him to condemn a fellow countryman. Rather,
he is called upon to judge Jesus as one on the outside, both eth-
nically and religiously. Can Pilate retain his neutrality?

Because Jesus' kingdom is not merely "an isolated sphere of
pure inwardness," nor "a private area for the cultivation of religious needs, which could not come into conflict with the world,"
but rather a word of judgment challenging the world's sin, he
cannot. A neutral stance toward Jesus is a decision against Jesus,
and in the end Pilate "does not have the strength to maintain the
standpoint which he had taken," but casts his lot with the
Jewish leaders and the world because he cannot take his stand
on the side of Jesus.[78]

3. Jesus. John's primary goal in his characterization of Jesus
throughout the passion narrative, including his Roman trial, is
the demonstration of his innocence of all the charges brought
against him by the Jewish leaders, including the central charge
of blasphemy (19:7). If Jesus is innocent, that is, negatively, if he
is "not guilty" as charged, it logically follows that, positively, he
is who he claimed to be, and who the fourth evangelist believes
him to be, namely the Christ, the Son of God (20:30-31). This

is how, on a larger scale, Jesus' trial before Pilate fits in with the purpose statement of John's Gospel. While Pilate in the present instance yields to the Jewish leaders, he, as the representative of Roman law, considers Jesus innocent (18:38; 19:4, 6), a fact that retains its significance despite the fact that Jesus ends up at the cross.

Since the passion narrative began in 18:1, Jesus has been betrayed by Judas (18:1-11), denied three times by Peter (18:15-18, 25-27), and interrogated by Annas the high priest (18:12-14, 19-24) and by Caiaphas (18:24, 28). Throughout the proceedings against him, Jesus is shown to maintain a calm demeanor. When those who would arrest him enter the garden, he steps forward and identifies himself as the one they have come to take into custody (18:4-5). When they hesitate, he identifies himself a second time in order to shield his followers from arrest (18:8-9). When Peter draws his sword and cuts off Malchus's ear, Jesus rebukes Peter and expresses his resolve to "drink the cup" the "Father has given" him (18:11).

When interrogated by Annas about his disciples and his teaching, Jesus responds that he always taught openly in the synagogues and in the temple; his teaching was no secret (18:20-21). At this, one of the officers standing by strikes Jesus with his hand, saying, "Is that how you answer the high priest?" (18:22). Again, Jesus retains his calm demeanor, responding only, "If what I said is wrong, bear witness about the wrong; but if what I said is right, why do you strike me?" Jesus has testified to the truth, and the truth is its own best defense. Neither hearing before Annas or Caiaphas leads to any charges being proven against Jesus, and with this Jesus is transferred to Pilate.

Now inside the governor's palace alone with Pilate, Jesus is asked by the governor whether or not he is "the king of the Jews."[79] Jesus is fully aware that the epithet "king of the Jews" is capable of more than one definition, especially given the different cultural, political, and religious backgrounds of Jews and Romans. As Darrell Bock points out, "If Pilate is asking from his own Roman interests, 'Do you have zealot-like designs against Caesar in an alternative political kingship?' then Jesus' reply would be negative. If he is asking from a Jewish perspective, 'Are you the promised Messiah?' then Jesus would respond positively."[80]

Hence, Jesus cannot simply answer Pilate's question; he must first define the sense in which he is and is not a king. Thus, with full composure, Jesus replies with a counter-question: "Do you say this of your own accord, or did others say it to you about me?" (18:34).[81] Jesus, of course, knows the answer (it was the latter), but he poses the question nonetheless in order to elicit Pilate's response to the Jewish leaders' charge before answering the governor's question himself. Pilate brusquely retorts, "Am I a Jew?" making it clear that it was the Jewish leaders who had presented Jesus to Pilate as a messianic pretender and political threat to Rome.

Then Jesus answers Pilate's question, yet he does so not in terms of his kingship, but of his kingdom.[82] Jesus' use of the term "kingdom" harks back both to Israel's monarchy under David and his successors and to the OT prophetic tradition, most notably Daniel (e.g., chaps. 2 and 7).[83] On a literary level in John's Gospel, Jesus' reference to his kingdom marks a critical shift from 3:3, 5: the kingdom of God has now become the kingdom of Jesus![84] Jesus' kingdom is not of this world: that is, it does not have its origin or derive its authorization from the world, but rather transcends the political and material sphere of this world.[85]

When Pilate probes further, "So you are a king?" (18:37; cf. 18:33), Jesus again does not provide a direct answer,[86] responding, "You say that I am a king" (18:37).[87] While not denying that he is a king, Jesus again does not focus on his own kingship but on the larger purpose for which he has come into the world: to bear witness to the truth (18:37).[88] The reader knows that Jesus is much more than a mere witness to the truth; he is the truth in his very own person. Yet, before Pilate, Jesus is humbly content to speak of his coming as a witness to the truth; to establish the reign of the truth and to witness to it—this is the purpose for which Jesus was born and has come into the world (18:37).

This truth, in turn, calls for a personal response: "Everyone who is of the truth listens to my voice" (18:37).[89] Within the framework of the Gospel, this statement echoes Jesus' words in his "Good Shepherd discourse" in chapter 10 (see vv. 3, 16, and esp. 27; see also 3:3, 21). In the context of the Johannine narrative, this echo may invoke the notion of Jesus as messianic shepherd who describes the nature of his kingship to the Roman governor.[90] While it is Jesus who is ostensibly the one being tried here, Jesus' words put the spotlight, at least momentarily, on Pilate: will he respond to the truth and listen to Jesus? Or will he listen to his accusers?[91] In principle, it would be possible for him to listen to Jesus. But responding to Jesus now would mean a radical break with his past, so radical that it is virtually unthinkable. Pilate's past enslaves him, and his present is too cluttered with political expediency and compromise to allow the truth to break through.[92] Like the Jewish leaders (10:26), Pilate is not among Jesus' "sheep." So, disappointingly but not surprisingly, after no more than perhaps a moment's hesitation, Pilate dismissively retorts, "What is truth?" and brusquely breaks off the interrogation, returning outside to render his verdict regarding Jesus to the Jewish leaders.[93]

After Jesus has endured a severe flogging and humiliation (19:1-6), and after the Jewish leaders have told Pilate that the real reason why they wanted Jesus crucified was that he had "made himself the Son of God" (19:7), Pilate, now afraid (cf. Matt. 27:19), summons Jesus one more time, asking him,

"Where are you from?" (19:9). But Jesus gives him no answer.[94]
The reader of the Gospel, of course, knows the answer—Jesus
is the eternal, preexistent Word of God (1:1)—but this truth
would be lost on Pilate.[95] Pilate, incredulous that the prisoner
would not take the opportunity to lobby the one who had
authority to free him for his release, asks Jesus, "You will not
speak to me? Don't you know that I have authority to release
you and authority to crucify you?" (19:10). But Jesus calmly
points out that Pilate's authority came "from above"—from
God—so that the one who delivered Jesus over to Pilate (presumably Caiaphas) was guilty of a greater sin.[96]

Hence throughout the entire proceedings against Jesus,
while Judas and Peter are hard-pressed and face inner turmoil,
while the Jewish leaders change their story and seek to cajole
and intimidate Pilate to render a "guilty" verdict concerning
Jesus, and while Pilate is quite literally torn between Jesus and
the Jewish leaders, Jesus stays calm, "knowing all that would
happen to him" (18:4), resolved to "drink the cup that the
Father has given" him (18:11). In fact, the Jewish leaders' seeking his death by crucifixion is shown "to fulfill the word that
Jesus had spoken to show by what kind of death he was going
to die" (18:32). In all of his suffering and humiliation, Jesus
respects the authority of Pilate and the Jewish leaders and
entrusts himself to God the Father.

As we assess the outcome and implications of Jesus' trial
before Pilate for Jesus, it is important to realize at the very outset that, in many ways, the present encounter is merely a culmi-
nation of preceding developments and dynamics. When Pilate
interrogated Jesus, he had behind him a life replete with political ruthlessness and compromise. His is a hardened conscience
and a willful rejection of truth. The Jewish leaders, too, have
shown in their response to Jesus' signs and teaching that they
will not listen to God's Messiah. The road that Jesus walked

prior to his appearance before Pilate, by contrast, was one of love, ministry to others, and uncompromising obedience to the One who sent him. In many ways, these three characters merely act out their part in a way that is consistent with their character and conduct up to that point.

How does Jesus fare in comparison to the Jewish leaders and Pilate? As mentioned above, both the Jewish leaders and Pilate temporarily emerge from the proceedings against Jesus in some sense victorious and yet fatally wounded. While the Jews' victory over Pilate and Jesus comes at the high cost of betraying their religious hope, and while Pilate agrees to condemn a man to die who he senses is innocent, Jesus, by contrast, the one who appears to be the major loser and victim of the Jewish leaders' and Pilate's "unprincipled alliance,"[97] has in fact not yielded anything, has ultimately lost nothing, and gained everything.

First of all, Jesus stayed true to his mission of testifying to the truth. He respected those whom God had put in authority over him and entrusted himself in faith to God the Father.

Second, Jesus fulfilled both the revelatory and the redemptive mission he had set out to accomplish (1:18; 4:34; 17:4; 19:31). On the cross, Jesus revealed the love of God for humankind (3:16) and as God's "Lamb" made atonement for sin (1:29, 36). Hence, according to Johannine theology, the cross, far from being a place of shame, became for Jesus a place of glory, the place where his perfect submission and obedience to the will of the Father were manifested, which included the provision of redemption for humankind.

Third, as John 20—21 make clear, Jesus rose from the dead on the third day, which marks the overruling of the Jewish plot to kill Jesus and Pilate's decision to condemn Jesus to die. Hence, in typical Johannine fashion, Jesus in the farewell discourse does not dwell on the imminent crucifixion but euphemistically subsumes it under his "return to the Father."

The way the fourth evangelist tells it, "when Jesus knew that his hour had come to depart out of this world to the Father, having loved his own who were in the world, he loved them to the end" (13:1). The cross merely marks Jesus' departure out of this world to the Father. Or as Jesus says in 14:12, believers will perform even greater works than he did subsequent to his departure, "because I am going to the Father." Listening to Jesus, it is as simple as that: "I came from the Father and have come into the world, and now I am leaving the world and going to the Father" (16:28)—barely a mention of the cross as a station on the way back to Jesus' place of glory with the Father (cf. 17:5, 24).

Though apparently the loser in the Jewish and Roman trials against him, Jesus thus emerges as the ultimate victor in the Gospel, eliciting from Pilate the acknowledgment that he (Pilate) was either indifferent to the truth or incapable of determining what it was (18:37-38a), plotting his strategy to spread his message of salvation (13—17), commissioning his followers as the Father had sent him (20:21), and calling Peter and the other disciples to follow him until he returns (21:19, 22). Pilate, on the other hand, as is known from subsequent history, continues to clash with his Jewish subjects and is recalled to Rome three short years after pronouncing the death sentence on Jesus.[98]

V. SUMMARY AND CONCLUDING OBSERVATIONS

Which results did our study of Jesus' trial before Pilate yield? First, we have seen that a strong case can be made for the historicity of John's account, both on the basis of the known history of Pilate's tenure in Palestine and of the pattern of Jesus' dealing with questions and representing his messianic calling to others. Second, we have seen that Pilate's question, "What is truth?" engages several major Johannine themes, including the trial motif, the theme of Jesus' kingship, and the notion of truth.

With regard to truth, we have noted the strong Christological orientation of truth in John's Gospel in line with the evangelist's purpose of proving that Jesus is the Christ and the Son of God. Third, the Jewish leaders, together with Jesus, were found to be the major characters in the present narrative, while Pilate turned out to be a comparatively minor figure.

I close with six observations from Jesus' trial before Pilate and a brief conclusion.

First, commentators regularly note the irony of Pilate's question, "What is truth?" in light of the fact that Truth incarnate, "the way, and the truth, and the life" (14:6), is standing right in front of him.[99] While not wanting to deny this, I believe there is an even more striking irony at work here. As Miroslav Volf aptly notes,

> Trials are supposed to be about finding out what happened and meting out justice. In Jesus' trial, neither the accusers nor the judge cared for the truth. . . . The judge scorns the very notion of truth: "What is truth?" he asks, and uninterested in any answer, he leaves the scene of dialogue. . . . For both the accusers and the judge, the truth is irrelevant because it works at cross-purposes to their hold on power. The only truth they will recognize is "the truth of power." It was the accused who raised the issue of truth by subtly reminding the judge of his highest obligation—find out the truth.[100]

In the context of the trial narrative, Pilate, as the one called to judge concerning the truth regarding Jesus, here dismisses the entire question of truth. If the judge cares nothing about the truth, what does that say about the value of Jesus' trial and the verdict reached regarding Jesus? The message is obvious: the question of truth was dismissed as glibly as Pilate's question dismissed Jesus' claim that he came to witness to the truth.

The second observation pertains to the parallelism maintained by the fourth evangelist regarding Caiaphas and Pilate, the Jewish high priest and the Roman governor. Both speak better than they know, Caiaphas, without realizing it, arguing for the necessity of Jesus' provision of substitutionary atonement (11:49-50; 18:14), Pilate unwittingly acknowledging Jesus as the truth (18:37). Both also share in their complicity in Jesus' death, Caiaphas as the one who handed Jesus over to Pilate (19:11), and Pilate in handing Jesus over to the Jews to have him crucified (19:16). In this momentous hour of salvation history, the evangelist therefore shows how these two characters are unequally yoked in the rejection of Jesus as the Messiah and "King of the Jews." Caiaphas's action on behalf of the Jewish nation and Pilate's action, representing the non-Jewish world, include Jew as well as non-Jew in the sin of crucifying the Truth. Whether by actively pursuing Jesus' death (the Jewish leaders) or by passively acquiescing to pressure (Pilate), the religious and political authorities in charge at the time of Jesus' trial conspired together against the Lord's anointed, as Psalm 2 envisages (vv. 1-2; cf. Acts 4:25-26), as evidence of the pervasive sinfulness engulfing a world that lies in darkness apart from the Light that has come in Jesus.

Third, Christologically and salvation-historically, truth is inextricably linked to the cross. In Jesus, the truth is crucified.[101] This does not mean the death of truth, for truth cannot be permanently kept down. Yet truth is intensely personal. It is Jesus who represents the truth in his very own person, and it is he who calls people to respond to him in faith. People's rejection of the truth, likewise, manifests itself in their rejection, not of a set of abstract propositions, but of Jesus. To employ the kind of reasoning John repeatedly uses in his first epistle, if anyone claims to love the truth and yet rejects Jesus, who is the Truth, how can that person legitimately claim to love the truth? In a world that often refers to God but rarely mentions Jesus, the fact that it is specifically in Jesus, rather than generically in God, that Truth is found is profoundly significant and intensely relevant. Not only this, but in this world, the truth, like Jesus, will always be called to suffer. The cross therefore ought to serve as a perennial reminder that, in this world, the only truth is a crucified truth. In this world, Jesus could not be the truth without ending up being called to die for the truth and as the truth. It will be the same for his followers.

Fourth, if the above analysis is on target, the two major characters or groups in the Johannine trial narrative are the Jewish leaders and Jesus, while Pilate turns out to be a comparatively minor character. As a character, Pilate only surfaces in John 18—19, and even there, he is continually shown to be torn in the clashing claims between the Jewish leaders and Jesus. By contrast, in the context of the Johannine narrative, both Jesus and the Jewish leaders pervade the story from beginning to end. The first clash between Jesus and the Jewish authorities occurs at the temple clearing in chapter 2 (vv. 14-22). It reaches its first major climax in chapter 5 (esp. v. 18) and continues to escalate, especially in chapters 8 and 10. Hence, even in chapters 18—19, while Pilate is temporarily in the foreground of the narrative, it is the Jewish leaders who have handed Jesus over to Pilate (18:30, 35-36) and who receive him back from Pilate to have him crucified (19:16).

The implication is that the Jews cannot blame Pilate for putting Jesus on the cross. The truth, certainly according to John's Gospel, is that they not only asked Pilate to render a "guilty" verdict regarding Jesus, but they exerted extensive pressure on Pilate to coerce him into compliance. This is not the place to defend John and his Gospel against the charge of anti-Semitism, nor does John need to be defended in this regard, since such charges are quite evidently anachronistic impositions of modern concerns onto the Gospel.[102] In the end, Jew and non-

"What Is Truth?" Pilate's Question in Its Johannine and Larger Biblical Context

49

Jew alike stand guilty before God in their complicity of rejecting the Messiah and the Truth, and every person stands in need
of responding to Jesus' vicarious death for humankind in personal faith.[103]

Fifth, what exactly was the tenor of Pilate's question, "What
is truth?" and why did he ask it? It seems that the major function of the question was that of cutting off Jesus' testimony, similar to the crowd's reaction to Paul's reference to Jesus'
resurrection in Acts 17:31. "No more—that's enough!" would
be a free, but, I believe, accurate reading of Pilate's intent. If
Pilate had meant his question, it would inquire, in good Roman
legal fashion, as to the actual facts of the case, in keeping with
his role as a judge in the matter. But Pilate did not intend to pro-
long the interrogation, nor did he display any real desire to get
to the bottom of the issue (contrast 7:17). No more talk of
"truth" and other philosophical gibberish. It was time to get on
to more important business.

Sixth and finally, Jesus' Roman trial speaks to the relationship between power and truth. If I may be allowed this anachro-
nism, the view of a lone, helpless prisoner before the
representative of imperial Roman power is not unlike the much
more recent image, broadcast all around the world, of the
Chinese student defying a tank at the demonstrations in
Tiananmen Square. Truth is pitted against power, and "the truth
of power" is pitted against "the power of truth."[104] Jesus' example shows that the power of truth does not depend on worldly
power—though ultimately in Jesus truth and power converge
(Rev. 11:15)—and in his willingness to die for the truth and for
others and in his refusal to resort to violence, he models "the
power of self-giving love."[105] Contrary to the claims of postmodernism, it is not true that the only truth there is is power.[106]
In this Jesus gives hope to all those who stand for truth and
because of this are oppressed by those in power.

VI. Conclusion

In the late 1970s, Václav Havel, writer, dissident, and more recently president of the Czech Republic, wrote an essay entitled, "An Attempt to Live in Truth: Of the Power of the Powerless."[107] This essay, which earned Havel an extended period in prison, is devoted to a critique of the totalitarianism that sent Soviet troops marching and tanks rolling down Wenceslas Square in Czechoslovakia's capital to crush the reform movement known as "Prague Spring." Havel recounts the story of a greengrocer who displays, together with his onions and carrots, a sign in his window, saying, "Workers of the world, unite!" Why, Havel asks, does the greengrocer display this sign? His answer: any political system that compels such an act of inauthenticity marks the rule of a lie. In fact, people's every action is a lie: voting in elections that are meaningless; listening to speeches that are inconsequential; saying the opposite of what they really think; posting an ideological slogan because they feel obliged to do so and because they do not want to get into trouble. This is what living a lie is all about.

But what would happen, Havel goes on to ask, if this greengrocer were to try and start living in the truth? If he were no longer to go to elections whose result was already predetermined? If he were no longer to participate in events that did nothing other than perpetrate stale ideologies? If he were to speak his mind rather than timidly parrot the beliefs of those in power? If he were no longer to cave in to the pressure to conform to the expectations of others? What would happen if he were to remove the slogan from his store window?

Havel knows firsthand what would happen. The recriminations Havel and his fellow dissidents experienced are a certainty for everyone who speaks up for the truth in the midst of a system of lies. But hear what Havel says about suffering for what a person knows to be true. There is no greater power than standing up for the truth, than simply speaking the truth, describing what one has seen, doing only what one believes he should do, living in keeping with one's faith, hope, and love. Living in the truth has tremendous personal and political consequences, which, once unleashed, have the potential of causing the collapse of an entire system of lies. In Havel's case, his words proved prophetic. The Iron Curtain fell, and the man who served repeatedly in prison for speaking up for the truth was appointed president of his country.

The same power of truth is evident in the lives of Jesus and his followers. Pilate's house of cards collapsed only three short years subsequent to Jesus' crucifixion, and, despite the Jewish leaders' efforts to keep the peace with Rome, their "place" was nonetheless destroyed in A.D. 70 and their "nation" laid waste (cf. 11:48). The rule of truth established by Jesus, on the other hand, took root, and, as the Book of Acts attests, the message of the resurrection spread like wildfire. The story of the early church gives powerful testimony to the fact that the truth cannot be permanently kept down.

Truth has a power of its own, a power that in the long run proves stronger than the usurped authority of institutional power. Jesus embodies this hope, the hope of the ultimate triumph of truth in the reign of his kingdom. It is this hope to which he bore witness in his "good confession" before Pontius Pilate. May you and I bear witness to this truth, the gospel, which is found only in Jesus, and may we, by our words and our lives, give a clear, distinct, and irrefutable answer to Pilate's question, "What is truth?"

2

TRUTH AND
CONTEMPORARY
CULTURE

R. Albert Mohler

*R. Albert Mohler, president of The Southern Baptist Theological
Seminary, Louisville, delivered this plenary address at the 56th annual
meeting of the Evangelical Theological Society on November 17, 2004, in
San Antonio, Texas.*

In 1999, Pulitzer Prize-winning historian and biographer
Edmund Morris released his much-anticipated work on
Ronald Reagan. Entitled *Dutch: A Memoir of Ronald Reagan*,
this novel—or biography, or biographical novel—set off a great
deal of controversy, not least among those who had hoped for
a successor to Morris's magisterial and quite factual, if interpretative, biography of Theodore Roosevelt.

Morris was quite upfront that his intention was to capture
Reagan's essence in a mixture of historical narrative, biographical interpretation—and fiction. His publisher, Random House,
even had the audacity to claim in its advertising that through
this device, Morris was merely telling the truth in an altogether
new way. Morris, himself the object of no small amount of crit-

icism, said concerning his project, "It was an advanced and bio-graphical honesty." In other words, by inventing a good per-centage of the biography, he had made the book more honest than it would otherwise have been.

We are living in an age of great confusion about the issue of truth. Ralph Keyes has authored a book entitled *The Post-Truth Era*, in which he suggests that society has now moved beyond a concern for truth. Truth has become such a contested category, he writes, that most persons go through life actually expecting to be lied to, to be the recipients of dishonesty, and to be confronted with endless misrepresentations by advertis-ers, cultural leaders, and now even biographers. In a world of media invention and virtual reality, truth has become a distant category to many persons, especially in the academic elite. Sociologist Jay A. Barnes, in his recent work on lying, suggests that people have grown so accustomed to untruth that many postmodernists now claim that lies are actually "meaningful data in their own right."[1]

Today, in sociological analysis, philosophical discussion, and of course political debate, the issue is truth itself. Recent debates over issues like embryonic stem cell research, same-sex marriage, sexuality, and human cloning are really disguised arguments about the nature of truth itself.

So what is truth? What is the true state of affairs in these sit-uations? What are the truth issues at stake? Whose truth will be victorious?

In every corner of culture, confusion and chaos run rampant in this post-truth age. In literature, for example, postmodern narrative has grown so minimalist that it has reached the point of having no point at all. As critic George Steiner explains, "God the Father of meaning in His authorial guise is gone from the game. There is no longer any privileged judge, interpreter, or explicator who can determine or communicate the truth, the true intent of the matter."[2] Similarly, artists, musicians, architects, and filmmakers have now openly embraced nihilism. There is, as one critic said, "a noticeable hole in the soul of our contemporary culture, both at its popular and elite levels." Objective meaning has been lost; whatever meaning and truth we find in the artifacts of culture, we are told, is brought there by the viewer in a subjective experience. Directors in the cinema industry now say that their sole ambition is to tell *their* truth, as if that were something different from *the* truth.

In large sectors of academia as well, truth has become such a contested category that no debate is more intense than whether truth can be known at all. The same is true in law, where truth is now a matter to be decided, not discovered. No longer does the nation's judicial system operate on the assumption that judges and juries will reach objective decisions after evaluating evidence presented in an objective manner.

How did we get here? Of course we could begin answering that question at almost any point in intellectual history, but we must begin at least with the Enlightenment. Modernist philosophers like Descartes, Locke, and Kant confronted Western culture with a series of tough questions—the problem of knowledge, most notably, and the subsequent postmodern hermeneutical shift to the subject. Such questions transformed the notion of truth in the Western mind.

The result was a confluence of movements all seeking to answer the question of how truth could be known. Rationalists and empiricists made their bids to ground human knowledge, and science began its growth toward intellectual hegemony as people embraced the myth of the objective, adopting the supposedly objective scientific method as the model for all knowledge. In the background to all this, of course, were those whom Paul Ricoeur called the "high priests and prophets of the hermeneutics of suspicion." Friedrich Nietzsche, Karl Marx,

Sigmund Freud, Charles Darwin, and their heirs intentionally attacked the reigning truth claims of the day in an effort to subvert them, transform them, and ultimately replace them with a very different understanding of reality.

Of course we cannot completely dispense with modernism, or see it as entirely hostile to the Christian faith. There were genuine gains in modernism that made possible everything from CAT scans to penicillin to microwave ovens to jet aircraft. The problem with the Enlightenment was the totalitarian imposition of the scientific model of rationality upon all truth, the claim that only scientific data can be objectively understood, objectively defined, and objectively defended. The loss in the wake of this modernist agenda was huge. It left Western culture with little more than a materialist worldview. However, in such a world of mere naturalistic materialism, what can truth possibly mean? In a letter to one of his colleagues, Darwin himself wondered about the effect of this very problem. "The horrid doubt always arises," he wrote, "whether the connection of the convictions of man's mind, which he has developed from the mind of lower animals, are of any value or at all trustworthy." He went on to ask, "Would anyone trust the convictions of a monkey's mind?"

In the United States, there was a quintessentially American response to this crisis, a system of thought known as pragmatism. In his work *The Metaphysical Club*, intellectual historian Louis Menand considers the influence of Oliver Wendell Holmes, William James, Charles Pierce, and John Dewey. He said of them: "These people had highly distinctive personalities, and they did not always agree with one another, but their careers intersected at many points, and together they were more responsible than any other group for moving American thought into the modern world."[3]

And what was the essential understanding of truth these men used to move America into the modern world? It was the idea that truth is a matter of social negotiation and that ideas are merely instrumental, tools whose truthfulness will be determined by whether or not they meet the particular needs of the present time. In the eyes of these pragmatists, ideas were nothing but provisional responses to actual challenges, and truth, by definition, was relative to the time, to the place, to the need, and to the person.

Oliver Wendell Holmes said this: "Men to a great extent believe what they want to," because it brings them self-satisfaction. William James applied this philosophy to psychology, and in particular to the psychology of religion. He suggested that truth is not something inherent to an idea, concept, or claim. Rather, he said, "Truth happens to an idea." John Dewey applied the same idea to public policy, education, and law. He insisted that the question, "Is it true?" really is not helpful at all, and should be replaced with the question, "Is it meaningful?"

Modernity thus presented the church of the Lord Jesus Christ with a significant intellectual crisis. As David Wells in his book *No Place for Truth* makes very clear, that crisis was the very questioning of whether truth can be known and taught and embraced and confessed at all.

We are now well aware that truth is stranger than it used to be. For modernism has been replaced by postmodernism—or if not replaced, then at least joined, for postmodernism, I will argue, is nothing more than the logical extension of modernism in a new mood. However one understands that shift, the theological community is confronted with a common concern when we understand the changed and strange Gestalt of the postmodern age. Much postmodern literature may be nonsensical and incomprehensible—and reads more like a vocabulary test than a sustained argument—but Christians cannot dismiss postmodernism as unimportant or irrelevant, for it is shaping the mind of the age, especially at the elite level. Therefore, it is a matter of concern not only to academics and the "elite guard," but to all those who care about the gospel of the Lord Jesus Christ.

On the question of truth in contemporary culture, the post-modern age confronts the church with a challenge of several dimensions. First, *a deconstruction of truth*. Truth has always been a matter of contention. Throughout all the centuries, even as far back as the pre-Socratic philosophers, truth was the major issue of philosophical concern and inquiry. Postmodernism, however, has turned this concern for truth on its head. While most arguments throughout history have been disputes between rival claims to truth, postmodernism rejects the very notion of truth as a fixed universal, or objective absolute. Modernist thinkers had earlier rejected revelation as a source of truth and, confident that their approach would yield objective and univer-sal truths by means of autonomous human reason, had attempted to establish truth on the basis of inductive thought and scientific investigation. Postmodernists reject both these approaches, arguing that neither revelation nor the scientific method is a reliable source for truth. According to postmodern theory, truth is not objective or absolute at all, nor can it be determined by any commonly accepted method. Instead, post-modernists argue that truth is socially constructed, plural, and inaccessible to universal reason, which itself does not exist any-way. As postmodern philosopher Richard Rorty asserts, "Truth is made rather than found."

According to the deconstructionists, an influential sect among the postmodernists, all truth is socially constructed. That is, social groups construct their own "truth" in order to serve their own interests. Michel Foucault, one of the most sig-nificant postmodern theorists, has argued that all claims to truth are constructed to serve those who are in power. Thus the root of the problem is the desire for power, and the role of the intellectual is to deconstruct truth claims in order to liberate the society. What has historically been understood and affirmed as truth, argue these postmodernists, is really nothing more than a convenient structure of thought intended to oppress the powerless. Truth is not universal, for every culture establishes its own. Neither is it objectively real, for all "truth" is merely constructed—or as Rorty would say, "made, not found."

Little imagination is needed to see that this radical relativism is a direct challenge to the Christian gospel. Our claim is not to preach one truth among many, about one savior among many, through one gospel among many. We do not believe that the Christian gospel is a socially constructed truth, but the truth that sets sinners free. It is objectively, historically, and universally true.

Second, *the death of the meta-narrative*. Because postmodernists believe all truth to be socially constructed, all claims of absolute, universal, and established truth must be resisted. All meta-narratives—that is, all grand and expansive accounts of truth, meaning, and existence—are cast aside, for they claim far more than they can deliver.

Jean-François Lyotard, perhaps the most famous European postmodernist, defined postmodernism simply as "incredulity toward meta-narratives."[4] Because they lay claim to universal truth, meta-narratives are oppressive, totalizing, hegemonistic, and thus to be resisted. Therefore, all the great philosophical systems are dead. All cultural accounts are limited. All that remains are little stories accepted as true by different groups and different cultures.

The problem with this, of course, is that Christianity is meaningless apart from the gospel, which is a meta-narrative, indeed the meta-narrative of meta-narratives. The Christian gospel is the great meta-narrative of redemption. Beginning with creation by the sovereign, omnipotent God, it continues through the fall of humanity into sin and the redemption of sinners through the substitutionary work of Christ on the cross, and promises a dual eternal destiny for all humanity—glory with God forever for the redeemed and everlasting punishment for the unredeemed. This message is irreducibly a meta-narrative. We do not preach the gospel as one narrative among many true narratives, or as merely our narrative alongside the authentic narratives of others. We cannot retreat to claims that biblical truth is merely true for us. For Christians to surrender the claim that the gospel is universally true and objectively established is to surrender the center of our faith. Our claim is that the Bible is the Word of God for all, a conviction that is deeply offensive to the postmodern worldview.

Third, *the demise of the text.* If the meta-narrative is dead, then the great texts behind those meta-narratives must also be dead. Postmodernism has declared it a fallacy to ascribe meaning to any text, or even to the author of a text. According to their thought, it is the reader of a text who establishes meaning, and there are no controls to limit the interpretation a reader might give. Jacques Derrida, the leading literary deconstructionist, described this move as the death of the author and the death of the text. Meaning is made, he taught, not found. It is created by the reader in the act of reading. Deconstructionists teach that the author must be removed from consideration and the text itself allowed to live as a liberating word.

This new hermeneutical method is no matter of mere academic significance. It explains much of our current debate in literature, politics, law, and theology. Deconstructionism stands behind much of the contemporary constitutional interpretation presented by judges and law professors, and it is also central to the fragmentation of modern biblical scholarship, the rise of the feminist liberation movement, the homosexual movement, and the way such issues are portrayed in the media.

According to the postmodern interpretive grid, every text must be deconstructed because every text contains a subtext of oppressive intentions on the part of the author. All texts, say the deconstructionists, from the United States Constitution to the works of Mark Twain, must be subjected to criticism and dissection, all in the name of liberation. Holy Scripture is no exception. Deconstructionists subject the Bible to radical reinterpretation, often with little or no regard for the plain meaning of the text or the clear intention of the human author. Some texts are simply identified as texts of terror, worthy only to be deconstructed so that humanity might be liberated from their tyranny. Any text that is not pleasing to the postmodern mind is rejected as suppressive, patriarchal, heterosexist, homophobic, "speciesist," or similarly deformed by some other political or ideological bias. The authority of the text is denied, and the most fanciful and even ridiculous interpretations are celebrated as affirming and therefore authentic.

Of course, the deconstructionist notion of the death of the author is particularly noxious when applied to Scripture, for Christians claim that the Bible is not merely the words of men, but the Word of God. Therefore postmodernism's insistence on the death of the author is inherently atheistic and antisupernaturalistic. In that, it continues the modernist project of subverting claims to revealed truth. Any claim to divine revelation is written off as only one more projection of oppressive power.

Fourth, *the dominion of therapy*. When truth is denied, therapy remains. The critical epistemological question is shifted from "What is true?" to "What makes me feel good?" What makes me feel authentic, healthy, and happy? This cultural trend has been developing for centuries, but it has now reached epic proportions. The culture we confront is almost completely under the foot of what Philip Rieff called "the triumph of the therapeutic." In a postmodern world, every issue eventually revolves around the autonomous self, and therefore enhanced self-esteem remains the goal of many educational and theological approaches. Categories like sin and morality are rejected as oppressive and harmful to self-esteem.

Therapeutic approaches have become dominant as a postmodern culture, made up of individuals uncertain whether truth even exists, tries to deal with the questions of the day. They are sure that self-esteem must remain intact, but there the clarity stops. Right and wrong are discarded as out-of-date reminders of an oppressive past, and all inconvenient moral standards are replaced with what Harvard Law professor Mary Ann Glendon calls "rights talk." There is no longer right and wrong, only rights.

Theology itself is likewise reduced to therapy. Entire theological systems are constructed with the goal of protecting and increasing the self-esteem of certain individuals and special groups. These feel-good theologies dispense with the "negativity" of orthodox Christianity and do away with any offensive biblical text or even with the Bible altogether. Out are categories such as lostness and judgment, and in their place are set vague notions of acceptance without repentance and wholeness without redemption. Adherents of such theologies may not know or even care if they are saved or lost, but they certainly do feel better about themselves.

Fifth, *the decline of authority*. Since postmodern culture is committed to such a radical vision of liberation, all authority must be overthrown. Texts, authors, traditions, meta-narratives, the Bible, God, and all powers in heaven and on earth must be dethroned. (Except, of course, for the high priests and apostles of the postmodern worldview who hold tenure in postmodern universities. They, of course, wield their power in the name of oppressed peoples everywhere.) According to the postmodernists, those in authority use their power simply to remain in power, to serve their own interests. Their laws, traditions, texts, and truth are nothing more than instruments designed to sustain them in power.

In such an intellectual atmosphere, the authority of governmental leaders is eroded, as is that of teachers, preachers, community leaders, and parents. In fact, the authority of God himself is ultimately rejected as totalizing, totalitarian, and autocratic. Furthermore, Christian ministers and Christian theologians, as representatives of this autocratic deity, are also resisted, while doctrines, traditions, creeds, and confessions are rejected as well and charged with limiting self-expression and representing oppressive authority.

Sixth, *the displacement of morality*. In Fyodor Dostoyevsky's novel *The Brothers Karamazov*, the character Ivan famously observed that if God is dead, then everything is permissible. The god allowed by postmodernism is not the God of the Bible; it is merely a vague idea of some spiritual reality. There are no tablets of stone, no Ten Commandments, no rules. Morality, along with the other foundations of culture, is discarded as inherently oppressive and totalitarian. A pervasive moral relativism marks postmodern culture. That is not to say that postmodernists are reluctant to employ moral language. On the contrary, they will often use the language of morality, but only in the hope of subverting a traditional moral code that they understand to be hegemonistic and oppressive. Postmodernists are typically quite arbitrary in their moral concerns, and in many cases their causes represent a reversal of biblical morality. Sexuality is central to this, and in many ways both modernism and postmodernism can be understood as lengthy and elaborate rationalizations for sexual misbehavior.

How should we think about all this? From the outset, we must recognize that postmodernism is something new, and yet not radically new. Essentially, it is the logical extension of some of the themes already present in modernism. It is modernity in its latest guise. Moreover, we must call attention to the fact that there is an awkwardness and a silliness to much postmodern discourse. Much of it is already dated, and quite frankly, no one is postmodern in the emergency room. When it comes to understanding objective truth, no one wants a postmodern heart surgeon. No one wants their CAT scans interpreted according to the particular anti-totalizing impulses of the surgeon. As Richard Dawkins once pithily noted, there are no postmodernists at 33,000 feet. Furthermore, modernism will not go away. It is still present in persons like Jürgen Habermas, who understands modernity as a project for human liberation and sees postmodernism as a threat to modernism's gains.

In the aftermath to all this, the question of truth is still being batted about as a topic of debate, like something of a ball for intellectual sport. Truth is reduced to Wittgensteinian language games, confined to what anthropologist Clifford Geertz described as "local knowledge" or "cultural linguistic systems." In this hard form, postmodernism assaults us with a barely disguised nihilism. For when everything is reduced to the interplay of words and language without external reference, when there is no truth that can be known and no reason with which to grasp such truth, then we lose all confidence in shared meaning and even in the communicability of truth itself.

Theologians, of course, have responded to the postmodern crisis. Our concern here is not so much with those who have embraced postmodernism openly and eagerly in its most extreme forms, but rather with those who have tried to find some means of incorporating its themes, mentality, and worldview into their theological systems. George Lindbeck and Hans Frei, for example, have appropriated both the Wittgensteinian understanding of language and the Geertzian understanding of culture to suggest that doctrine is a matter of grammatical rules. Also to be noted are the projects by Stanley Hauerwas, the late John Howard Yoder, and British philosopher Alasdair MacIntyre. In these we have seen the development of something like a new-style neo-orthodoxy, which emphasizes the believing community and construes doctrine as the practice and social embodiment of the church. Having embraced much of the direction and trajectory of modernism, these theologians call themselves "postliberal" and consider themselves to be literally beyond liberalism. That does not mean, however, that they have come to some conservative understanding, nor have they embraced any kind of evangelical identity. Nevertheless, they do understand that the acids of modernity, and the absolute confusion of postmodernity to which modernity gave birth, have left the church without a distinctive voice or a distinctive message.

How have evangelicals responded to this crisis of truth in contemporary culture? Many have openly celebrated the rise of the postmodern age, redefining themselves as revisionists, reformists, post-conservatives, or even post-evangelicals. Philip D. Kenneson welcomed the postmodern worldview with the title of his book, *There is No Such Thing as Objective Truth, and It Is a Good Thing, Too*, as did J. Richard Middleton and Brian F. Walsh with their *Truth Is Stranger Than It Used to Be*. Kenneson said of postmodernism, "We need to embrace this" and move beyond what he calls "the truth question." The sooner we do so, he says, "the sooner we can get on with being Christian, which in no way entails accepting a certain philosophical account of truth, justification and 'reality.'"[5]

Yet therein lies the question: is it really the case that Christianity does not entail accepting a certain philosophical account of truth, justification, and reality? Does our culture's denial of truth and its increasing embrace of the postmodern worldview mean that evangelicals must abandon their historic theological paradigm?

Some, referring to themselves as post-conservative evangelicals, have argued that indeed postmodernism represents a significant challenge to evangelical theology, but a challenge largely to be embraced. They argue forthrightly that Christians ought to embrace postmodernism, and the sooner the better. Variously engaged in different post-conservative movements are individuals like Stanley Grenz, Gary Dorrien, Henry Knight, John Franke, Roger Olsen, Clark Pinnock, and William Abraham.

I would suggest that these post-conservative evangelicals make two assertions related to the issue of truth in our contemporary culture. First, there is the negative claim that the classical evangelical paradigm, with its focus on revelation, propositional truth, and issues like biblical inerrancy, is a form of modernism—an evangelical variant of the Enlightenment project and, they would argue, a failed evangelical attempt at foundationalism. Second, there is the positive argument that an open embrace of at least part of the postmodern project—if not the whole of it—will lead to a great apologetic breakthrough and theological advance for the evangelical movement.

Central to this diagnosis is the presumed failure of foundationalism. In a recently released book entitled *Reclaiming the Center*, philosophers J. P. Moreland and Garrett DeWeese argue in a chapter called "The Premature Report of Foundationalism's Demise" that three theoretical commitments are held in common by most post-conservatives: first, the rejection of the correspondence theory of truth in favor of an epistemic or deflationary theory of truth; second, the rejection of metaphysical realism in favor of a theory of socially or linguistically constructed reality; and third, the rejection of the referential theory of language in favor of a semiotic theory in which linguistic signs refer only to other signs, and never to the world as it is.

One of the clearest and most lucid representatives of this post-conservative mood is Stanley Grenz, who writes,

The contemporary rejection of foundationalism offers evangelical theologians a great challenge as well as a providential opportunity. The dislocation of the present, together with the quest to move beyond the older foundationalist epistemology, places them [that is, evangelical theologians] in a position to realize how dependent neo-evangelical theology has been on an Enlightenment paradigm, and how decreasingly appropriate this approach is in a world that is increasingly post-theological.[6]

Two significant moves are made here. The first is to embrace the postmodern epistemological crisis as normative, meaning that hierarchies of truth, metaphysical realism, correspondence theories of truth, and propositions are rejected, as well as any understanding of the Bible as our ultimate epistemological foundation. The second move is to criticize the received evangelical tradition as neo-evangelical, and to identify evangelical theologians—Carl Henry and Millard Erickson, for example—as conservative modernists and biblical foundationalists. According to the post-conservative evangelicals, it was Henry who introduced a thoroughgoing rationalism and thoroughgoing propositionalism into the "still fluid goo" of the emerging evangelical theology, a mistake they say the church would do well to reverse.[7]

There is no doubt that the postmodern age, just as much as the modern age, demands of the church, and of evangelical theology in particular, some serious thinking, critical engagement, and honest confrontation. In speaking of truth in contemporary culture, however, and in relating it to the future of evangelical theology at large, there is a need not only for honesty, but for decision. We are faced today with two trajectories for the future of evangelical theology, two paradigms of truth and theology, two competing apologetics, two readings of evangelical history, two (or at least two) definitions of evangelical identity, and two models for engaging the culture. As we look into the twenty-first century, we are making significant decisions about which understanding of evangelicalism and which evangelical theology will be handed to the next generation.

The post-conservatives are right to say we must engage the worldview of this age. We need to understand postmodernism. We need to take into account the postmodern turn, but we must also understand that it is still turning. In terms of its ideological shape, postmodernism is still largely confined to an academic elite, even though its nihilistic mood and themes are filtering down into popular culture. Yet in their daily lives, most people still hold to something like a correspondence theory of truth. They still have confidence in the existence of absolute truth and objective reality, and their lives would be unworkable—practically impossible—without it.

Despite the very real intellectual challenge presented to us by postmodernism, I believe it has fatally overreached. First, its outright rejection of foundationalism is untenable. For how are we to understand thought itself without some form—at least a soft form—of foundationalism? Even anti-foundationalists end up with some kind of foundationalism, nuanced and minimal though it may be. Even anarchist groups have leaders. Thought has to begin somewhere, and if there is to be any orderly process of thought, that beginning must be clearly articulated and understood as having some authority. It must be, at least in some sense, at the top of a hierarchy of ideas, and logically prior to all other ideas.

Second, the anti-realism of postmodern theology is faced with severe limitations, and is thus unsustainable. Some correspondence understanding of truth is inherent to every important truth claim. Once again, we could not operate in everyday life without a basic dependence upon a correspondence theory of truth. Furthermore, there is no way to preach the gospel of the Lord Jesus Christ, nor to describe the contours and substance of the gospel itself, without obviously implying some kind of correspondence. This is not to suggest that correspondence is dependent upon the modernist understanding of truth. It is rather a natural way of talking that allows us to proclaim the faith once for all delivered to the saints, to make truth claims just as the apostles made truth claims, and to speak boldly with the assurance that we are speaking about an objective, transcendent, and revealed reality. We are left finally with what Robert Alston referred to as "eolithic realism," the absolutely basic awareness that truth, language, and ideas express something other than interiority, and refer to something outside themselves. Furthermore, it is very hard to get by without propositions, despite the hostility directed toward them by postmodernists. Just as anarchist groups have leaders, anti-propositionalist writers themselves use propositions, paragraph by paragraph, to make their arguments. Our minds are made to use propositions, and that is not—to counter Darwin—merely an evolutionary accident. It is a testimony to the fact that our Creator who made us in his image has created us with a mental capacity and rationality that requires propositional formation.

The way out of this hermeneutical nihilism and metaphysical anti-realism is the doctrine of revelation. It is indeed the evangelical, biblical doctrine of revelation that breaks this epistemological impasse and becomes the foundation for a revelatory epistemology. This is not foundationalism in a modernist sense. It is not rationalism. It is the understanding that God has spoken to us in a reasonable way, in language we can understand, and has given us the gift of revelation, which is his willful disclosure of himself, the forfeiture of his personal privacy.

Post-conservative evangelicals employ a fallacious reading of evangelical history here. The evangelical paradigm never was rationalistic in the sense of claiming an autonomous reason. Nor was it true foundationalism in the sense of establishing a plat-

form for thought independent of God's revelation. At the very
heart of the evangelical movement, indeed from the very beginning, is a confidence in the God who speaks. Evangelicals have
always believed and taught that it is God's revelation that brings
us out of hermeneutical and epistemological nihilism and into a
world of true meaning. It is not autonomous human reason, but
the Bible that is the error-free, incontrovertible foundation for
all evangelical theology. Steven J. Wellum expressed this well:
"A scriptural foundationalism is not grounded in the finite
human subject as both modernism and postmodernism attempt
to do, but instead it is rooted and grounded in the Bible's own
presentation of the triune God."[8]

Of course, some genuine insights have come from the
engagement of evangelical theology and evangelical theologians
with the postmodern worldview. The necessity of understanding community, for example, is one. God does not address truth
to isolated, autonomous individuals, but rather to the church,
to his redeemed people. There is also gain in understanding the
sociological and anthropological embeddedness of all human
beings, both individually and in communities, as well as in
understanding the crucial role of the Holy Spirit, combined with
the Word. All this could lead to a healthful renaissance in eccle-
siology, but only if the church is understood to be the product
of the divine revelation, and not the producer of the divine revelation. Revelation—the in-breaking of the transcendent,
sovereign God into our finite and fallen world—must be our
epistemological principle, the ground of all our claims to know
what is really real and truly true.

Looking back at the history of the evangelical movement,
and remembering the intellectual crises our forefathers and fore-
mothers faced, we see that every generation lives in a particular
time that demands a particular response. As we face our own
challenges in this generation, we can always say more than they

did, but we can never say less. Of course truth is more than propositional, but it can never be less than propositional. Of course truth is more than can fit within any correspondence theory, but it can never be less than that which corresponds to the divine reality. When we consider our creeds, confessions, and doctrinal statements, it is always possible—indeed it is necessary—to say more, but we must never say less. We do not want mere propositions, nor mere rationality, but neither do we want anything less than reasoned understanding of the propositions revealed in Scripture.

Carl F. H. Henry defined theology in these terms:

> Divine revelation is the source of all truth, the truth of Christianity included. Reason is the instrument for recognizing. Scripture is its verifying principle. Logical consistency is a negative test for truth, and coherence a subordinate test. The task of Christian theology is to exhibit the content of divine revelation as an orderly whole.[9]

Everything Henry says here is accurate and true. He rightly defines and distills an evangelical theological method. Is there more to it than that? Of course there is. That is why we worship and why, even as we use words in worship, we confess that the truth of the one true and living God is so much greater than can be expressed in words. But that truth cannot be expressed in less than words. It cannot be formulated in less than propositions. We can certainly say more than Henry said, but we cannot say anything less.

I fear there are some who would wish to say less, to embrace the themes of the postmodern movement and the postmodern mood in such a way as to create a new paradigm for evangelicalism. This new trajectory would be so de-propositionalized, so epistemologically nuanced that it would have us embrace a queasy postmodern uncertainty about the very certainties that have defined the evangelical movement from the beginning. We would thus become liberals who arrive late, and there would be no methodological controls at all upon what would be acceptable among us.

It is easy to sympathize with those who hope for a theological third way, because it is easy to predict the censure, outrage, and dismissal that will come from the academic elite when they finally comprehend what we are saying. But that is a scandal we are called to bear. If it was a scandal from the beginning of the evangelical movement, why should we think it would be popular now?

In his review of Gary Dorrien's book *The Remaking of Evangelical Theology*, John G. Stackhouse wrote:

> Evangelicalism is a network and tradition of Christians united in a few select convictions. As such, evangelicalism is not essentially committed to this or that theological method, so long as Christ is glorified, the Bible obeyed, the gospel preached, and the Kingdom extended.[10]

That is wishful thinking. Evangelicals are committed to a theological method that understands truth to be something more than the postmodernist can ever understand or embrace. Truth is revealed in Scripture. Truth is revealed in the One who said, "I am the way, the truth, and the life." Truth is revealed in Jesus Christ, who prayed that his Father would sanctify his own in the truth and who confessed, "Thy word is truth." That is something far beyond what the postmodern mood, movement, or Gestalt can ever comprehend or accept.

Contemporary culture presents us with a challenge, but in essence it is the same challenge that has confronted the church all along. We still stand where Paul stood in Acts 17. We have to give the same answer he gave. If we as evangelicals are not committed to a theological method with a robust understanding of truth, there is a great and imminent danger that Christ will not in fact be glorified, the Bible will not be obeyed, the gospel will not be preached, and the Kingdom will not be extended. Let us therefore be determined to be a people who will say more, but who will never say less.

TRUTH, CONTEMPORARY PHILOSOPHY, AND THE POSTMODERN TURN

J. P. Moreland

*J. P. Moreland, professor of philosophy of religion at Biola University, La
Mirada, California, delivered this plenary address at the 56th annual
meeting of the Evangelical Theological Society on November 18, 2004, in
San Antonio, Texas.*

It is difficult to think of a topic of greater concern than the nature of truth. Indeed, truth and the knowledge thereof are the very rails upon which people ought to live their lives. And over the centuries the classic correspondence theory of truth has outlived most of its critics. But these are postmodern times, or so we are often told, and the classic model, once ensconced deeply in the Western psyche, must now be replaced by a neo-pragmatist or some other anti-realist model of truth, at least for those concerned with the rampant victimization raging all around us. Thus, "we hold these truths to be self-evident" now reads, "our socially constructed selves arbitrarily agree that certain chunks of language are to be esteemed in our linguistic community." Something has gone wrong here, and paraphrasing the words of *Mad* magazine's Alfred E. Newman, "We came, we saw, and we conked out!"

The astute listener will have already picked up that I am an unrepentant correspondence advocate who eschews the various anti-realist views of truth. In what follows I shall weigh in on the topic, first, by sketching out the correspondence theory and the postmodern rejection of it, and, second, by identifying five confusions of which I believe postmodern revisionists are guilty. I shall close by warning that not only are postmodern views of truth and knowledge confused, but postmodernism is an immoral and cowardly viewpoint that people who love truth and knowledge, especially disciples of the Lord Jesus, should do everything they can to heal.

I. WHAT IS THE CORRESPONDENCE THEORY OF TRUTH?

In its simplest form, the correspondence theory of truth says that a proposition is true just in case it corresponds to reality, when what it asserts to be the case is the case. More generally, truth obtains when a truth-bearer stands in an appropriate correspondence relation to a truth-maker:

correspondence relation

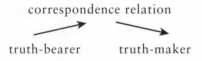

truth-bearer   truth-maker

Certain clarifications are called for. First, what is a truth-bearer? The thing that is either true or false is not a sentence, statement, or other piece of language, but a proposition. A proposition is, minimally, the content of a sentence. For example, "It is raining" and "*Es regnet*" are two different sentences that express the same proposition. A sentence is a linguistic object consisting in a sense-perceptible string of markings formed according to a culturally arbitrary set of syntactical rules, a grammatically well-formed string of spoken or written scratchings/sounds. Sentences are true just in case they express a true proposition or content. We will return to the topic of propositions later.

What about truth-makers? What is it that makes a proposition true? The best answer is facts. A fact is some real—that is, obtaining—state of affairs in the world—for example, grass's being green, an electron's having a negative charge, God's being all-loving. For present purposes, this identification of the truth-maker will do, but the account would need to be filled out to incorporate future states of affairs that will obtain or counterfactual states of affairs that would have obtained given such and such. Returning to present purposes, consider the proposition that grass is green. This proposition is true just in case a specific fact, viz., grass's being green, actually obtains in the real world. If Sally has the thought that grass is green, the specific state of affairs (grass actually being green) "makes" the propositional content of her thought true just in case the state of affairs actually is the way the proposition represents it to be. Grass's being green makes Sally's thought true even if Sally is blind and cannot tell whether or not it is true, and even if Sally does not believe the thought. Reality makes thoughts true or false. A thought is not made true by someone believing it or by someone being able to determine whether or not it is true. Put differently, evidence allows one to tell whether or not a thought is true, but the relevant fact is what makes it true. It goes without saying that "makes" in "a fact makes a proposition true" is not causal but rather is a substitution instance of "in virtue of"—the proposition is true in virtue of the fact.

Our study of truth-bearers has already taken us into the topic of the correspondence relation. Correspondence is a two-placed relation between a proposition and a relevant fact that is its intentional object. A two-placed relation, such as "larger than," is one that requires two things (say, a desk and a book) before it holds. Similarly, the truth relation of correspondence holds between two things—a relevant fact and a proposition—just in case the fact matches, conforms to, corresponds with the proposition.

II. WHY BELIEVE THE CORRESPONDENCE THEORY?

What reasons can be given for accepting the correspondence theory of truth? Many are available, but the simplest is the descriptive argument. The descriptive argument focuses on a careful description and presentation of specific cases of coming to experience truth to see what can be learned from them about truth itself. As an example, consider the case of Joe and Frank. While in his office, Joe receives a call from the university bookstore that a specific book he had ordered—Richard Swinburne's *The Evolution of the Soul*—has arrived and is waiting for him. At this point, a new mental state occurs in Joe's mind—the thought that Swinburne's *The Evolution of the Soul* is in the bookstore.

Now Joe, being aware of the content of the thought, becomes aware of two things closely related to it: the nature of the thought's intentional object (Swinburne's book being in the bookstore) and certain verification steps that would help him determine the truth of the thought. For example, he knows that it would be irrelevant for verifying the thought to go swimming in the Pacific Ocean. Rather, he knows that he must take a series of steps that will bring him to a specific building and look in certain places for Swinburne's book in the university bookstore.

So Joe starts out for the bookstore, all the while being guided by the proposition that Swinburne's *The Evolution of the Soul* is in the bookstore. Along the way, his friend Frank joins him, though Joe does not tell Frank where he is going or why. They arrive at the store and both see Swinburne's book there.

At that moment Joe and Frank simultaneously have a certain sensory experience of seeing Swinburne's book *The Evolution of the Soul*. But Joe has a second experience not possessed by Frank. Joe experiences that his thought matches and corresponds with an actual state of affairs. He is able to compare his thought with its intentional object and "see," be directly aware of, the truth of the thought. In this case Joe actually experiences the correspondence relation itself, and truth itself becomes an object of his awareness. "Truth" is ostensibly defined by this relation Joe experiences.

III. POSTMODERNISM AND TRUTH

Postmodernism is a loose coalition of diverse thinkers from several different academic disciplines. So it is difficult to characterize postmodernism in a way that would be fair to this diversity. Still, it is possible to provide a fairly accurate characterization of postmodernism in general, since its friends and foes understand it well enough to debate its strengths and weaknesses.[1]

As a philosophical standpoint, postmodernism is primarily a reinterpretation of what knowledge is and what counts as knowledge. More broadly, it represents a form of cultural relativism about such things as reality, truth, reason, value, linguistic meaning, the self, and other notions. On a postmodernist view, there is no such thing as objective reality, truth, value, reason, and so forth. All these are social constructions, creations of linguistic practices, and as such are relative not to individuals, but to social groups that share a narrative.

Postmodernism denies the correspondence theory, claiming that truth is simply a contingent creation of language that expresses customs, emotions, and values embedded in a community's linguistic practices. For the postmodernist, if one claims to have the truth in the correspondence sense, this assertion is a power move that victimizes those judged not to have the truth.

IV. FIVE CONFUSIONS THAT PLAGUE POSTMODERNISM

According to Brian McLaren, making absolute truth claims becomes problematic in the postmodern context. Says McLaren, "I think that most Christians grossly misunderstand the philosophical baggage associated with terms like *absolute* or *objective* (linked to foundationalism and the myth of neutrality). . . . Similarly, arguments that pit absolutism versus relativism, and objectivism versus subjectivism, prove meaningless or absurd to postmodern people. . . ."[2] McLaren not only correctly identifies some central postmodern confusions, but his statement indicates that he exhibits some of the confusions himself. Let us try to unpack some of the philosophical baggage to which McLaren refers and bring some clarity to the confusion.

1. *Metaphysical vs. epistemic notions of absolute truth.* The first postmodern confusion involves metaphysical vs. epistemic notions of absolute truth. In the metaphysical and correct sense, absolute truth is the same thing as objective truth. On this view, people discover truth, they do not create it, and a claim is made true or false in some way or another by reality itself, totally independently of whether the claim is accepted by anyone. Moreover, an absolute truth conforms to the three fundamental laws of logic, which are themselves absolute truths. According to objectivism, a commitment to the absolute truth of some proposition P entails no thesis about a knowing subject's epistemic situation regarding P.

By contrast with the metaphysical notion, postmodernists claim that a commitment to absolute truth is rooted in Cartesian anxiety and its need for absolute certainty and, accordingly, claim that acceptance of the absolute truth of P entails acceptance of the conjunction of P's truth in the objective sense and the possibility of a (finite) knowing subject having Cartesian certainty with respect to P. Thus, one postmodernist recently opined that commitment to objective truth and the correspondence theory is merely ". . . an epistemic project [that] is funded by 'Cartesian anxiety,' a product of methodological doubt. . . ."[3]

As I have already pointed out, this claim is entirely false philosophically. Advocates of a correspondence theory of objective truth take the view to be a realist metaphysical thesis, and they steadfastly reject all attempts to epistemologize the view. Moreover, historically it is incredible to assert that the great Western thinkers from Aristotle up to Descartes—correspondence advocates all—had any concern whatever about truth and Cartesian anxiety. The great correspondence advocate Aristotle was hardly in a Cartesian quandary when he wisely pointed out that in the search for truth, one ought not expect a greater degree of epistemic strength than is appropriate to the subject matter, a degree of strength that varies from topic to topic. The correspondence theory was not born when Descartes came out of his stove, and postmodernists lose credibility when they pretend otherwise.

2. *Two confusions about epistemic objectivity.* Postmodernists also reject the notion that rationality is objective on the grounds that no one approaches life in a totally objective way without bias. Thus, objectivity is impossible, and observations, beliefs, and entire narratives are theory-laden. There is no neutral standpoint from which to approach the world. Therefore, observations, beliefs, and so forth are perspectival constructions that reflect the viewpoint implicit in one's own web of beliefs. For example, Stanley Grenz claims that postmodernism rejects the alleged modernist view of reason that ". . . entails a claim to dispassionate knowledge, a person's ability to view reality not as a conditioned participant but as an unconditioned observer—to peer at the world from a vantage point outside the flux of history."[4]

Regarding knowledge, postmodernists believe that there is no point of view from which one can define knowledge itself without begging the question in favor of one's own view. "Knowledge" is a construction of one's social, linguistic structures, not a justified, truthful representation of reality by one's mental states. For example, knowledge amounts to what is deemed to be appropriate according to the professional certification practices of various professional associations. As such, knowledge is a construction that expresses the social, linguistic structures of those associations, nothing more, nothing less.

These postmodernist claims represent some very deep confusions about the notion of objectivity. As a first step toward clearing away this confusion, we need to draw a distinction between psychological and rational objectivity. It is clear from the quote above that Grenz's confused understanding of objectivity is at least partly rooted in his mistaken conflation of these two senses. Psychological objectivity is detachment, the absence of bias, a lack of commitment either way on a topic.

Do people ever have psychological objectivity? Yes, they do, typically in areas in which they have no interest or about which they know little or nothing. Note carefully two things about psychological objectivity. For one thing, it is not necessarily a virtue. It is if one has not thought deeply about an issue and has no convictions regarding it. But as one develops thoughtful, intelligent convictions about a topic, it would be wrong to remain "unbiased," that is, uncommitted regarding it. Otherwise, what role would study and evidence play in the development of one's approach to life? Should one remain "unbiased" that cancer is a disease, that rape is wrong, that the New Testament was written in the first century, that there is design in the universe, if one has discovered good reasons for each belief? No, one should not.

What is more, while it is possible to be psychologically objective in some cases, most people are not psychologically objective regarding the vast majority of the things they believe.

In these cases, it is crucial to observe that a lack of psychological objectivity does not matter, nor does it cut one off from knowing or seeing the world directly the way it is, or from presenting and arguing for one's convictions. Why? Because a lack of psychological objectivity does not imply a lack of rational objectivity, and it is the latter than matters most, not the former.

To understand this, we need to get clear on the notion of rational objectivity. Rational objectivity is the state of having accurate epistemic access to the thing itself. This entails that if one has rational objectivity regarding some topic, then one can discern the difference between genuinely good and bad reasons/evidence for a belief about that topic and one can hold the belief for genuinely good reasons/evidence. The important thing here is that bias does not stand between a knowing subject and an intentional object, nor does it eliminate a person's ability to assess the reasons for something. Bias may make it more difficult, but not impossible. If bias made rational objectivity impossible, then no teacher—including the postmodernist herself—could responsibly teach any view the teacher believed on any subject! Nor could the teacher teach opposing viewpoints, because she would be biased against them!

We will return below to the topic of cognitive access to the objects of consciousness, but for now I simply note that Grenz exhibits the twin confusions, so common among postmodernists, of failing to assess properly the nature and value of psychological objectivity and of failing to distinguish and properly assess the relationship between psychological and rational objectivity.

3. *Confusions between classical foundationalism and foundationalism per se.* Postmodernists reject foundationalism as a theory of epistemic justification. For example, as they assert "the demise of foundationalism," Stanley Grenz and John Franke observe with irony, "How infirm the foundation."[5]

Rodney Clapp claims that foundationalism has been in "dire straits" for some time, avowing that "few if any careful thinkers actually rely on foundationalist thinking," even though they cling like addicted smokers to "foundationalist rhetoric." Says Clapp, evangelicals "should be nonfoundationalists exactly because we are evangelicals."[6] Nancey Murphy is concerned to justify a "postmodern" theological method in the face of "a general skeptical reaction to the demise of foundationalism in epistemology."[7]

A major reason for this rejection is the idea that foundationalism represents a quest for epistemic certainty, and it is this desire to have certainty that provides the intellectual impetus for foundationalism. This so-called Cartesian anxiety is alleged to be the root of foundationalist theories of epistemic justification. But, the argument continues, there is no such certainty, and the quest for it is an impossible one. Further, that quest is misguided, because people do not need certainty to live their lives well. Sometimes Christian postmodernists support this claim by asserting that the quest for certainty is at odds with biblical teaching about faith, the sinfulness of our intellectual and sensory faculties, and the impossibility of grasping an infinite God.

Unfortunately, this depiction of the intellectual motives for foundationalism represents a confusion between foundationalism per se and an especially extreme Cartesian form of foundationalism, with the result that versions of modest foundationalism are simply not taken into consideration. To see this, note that "foundationalism" refers to a family of theories about what kinds of grounds constitute justification for belief, all of which hold the following theses:

(1) A proper noetic structure is *foundational*, composed of properly basic beliefs and non-basic beliefs, where non-basic beliefs are based either directly or indirectly on properly basic

beliefs, and properly basic beliefs are non-doxastically grounded, that is, not based entirely on other beliefs;

(2) The basing relation that confers justification is irreflexive and asymmetrical; and

(3) A properly basic belief is a belief that meets some Condition C, where the choice of C marks different versions of foundationalism.

Classical foundationalism, of which the Cartesian project is the paradigm example, holds that Condition C is indubitability (or some relevantly similar surrogate): the ground of the belief must guarantee the truth of the belief. It is recognized in nearly all quarters that classical foundationalism is too ambitious. Even granting, as I certainly would, that there are some indubitable beliefs, there simply are not enough of them to ground our entire noetic structure. Further, it clearly seems that certain beliefs that are not indubitable may legitimately be held as properly basic—for example, beliefs grounded in perception, memory, or testimony. What is more, classical foundationalism is motivated largely by the belief that certainty is a necessary condition of knowledge, or that one must know that one knows in order to have knowledge. But these analyses are either too strict or lead to an infinite regress, leading in either case to the skeptic's lair.

In point of fact, the past three decades have witnessed the development of various versions of foundationalism that avoid the criticisms leveled against the classical version. Among contemporary epistemologists, modest foundationalism of some form is, as one philosopher put it, the "dominant position."[8]

Thus, it is intellectually irresponsible for Clapp, Murphy, and others to claim that foundationalism is losing favor among philosophers. As far as I can tell, apart from intellectual dishonesty, this false viewpoint can be sustained only by conflating classical foundationalism with foundationalism per se, but this is simply mistaken, as the widespread acceptance of modest foundationalism makes clear. Modest foundationalism holds that Condition C is something weaker than indubitability: the ground of the belief must be truth-conducive. Thus at least some properly basic beliefs in a modest foundationalism are defeasible (subject to being shown to be false by subsequent evidence).

4. *Confusions about the identity of the truth-bearer.* As we have already seen, the informed correspondence theorist will say that propositions are truth-bearers. What is a proposition? Minimally, it is the content of declarative sentences/statements and thoughts/beliefs that is true or false. Beyond that philosophers are in disagreement, but most would agree that a proposition (1) is not located in space or time; (2) is not identical to the linguistic entities that may be used to express it; (3) is not sense-perceptible; (4) is such that the same proposition may be in more than one mind at once; (5) need not be grasped by any (at least finite) person to exist and be what it is; (6) may itself be an object of thought when, for example, one is thinking about the content of one's own thought processes; (7) is in no sense a physical entity.

By contrast a sentence is a linguistic type or token consisting in a sense-perceptible string of markings formed according to a culturally arbitrary set of syntactical rules. A statement is a sequence of sounds or body movements employed by a speaker to assert a sentence on a specific occasion. So understood, neither sentences nor statements are good candidates for the basic truth-bearer.

It is pretty easy to show that having or using a sentence (or any other piece of language) is neither necessary nor sufficient for thinking or having propositional content. First, it is not necessary. Children think prior to their acquisition of language—how else could they thoughtfully learn language—and, indeed, we all think without language regularly. Moreover, the same propositional content may be expressed by a potentially infinite number of pieces of language, and thus that content is not identical to any linguistic entity. This alone does not show that language is not necessary for having propositional content. But when one attends to the content that is being held constant as arbitrary linguistic expressions are selected to express it, that content may easily be seen to satisfy the non-linguistic traits of a proposition listed above.

Second, it is not sufficient. If erosion carved an authorless linguistic scribble in a hillside—for example, "I am eroding"—then strictly speaking it would have no meaning or content, though it would be empirically equivalent to another token of this type that would express a proposition were it the result of authorial intent.

Postmodernists attack a straw man when they focus on the alleged inadequacies of linguistic objects to do the work required of them in a correspondence theory of truth. Speaking for himself and other postmodernists, Joseph Natoli claims that "[n]o one representation, or narrative, can reliably represent the world because language/pictures/sounds (signifiers) are not permanent labels attached to the things of the world nor do the things of the world dwell inside such signifiers."[9] Unfortunately, even granting the fact that language (and certain sensations) is problematic if taken to represent things in the world (e.g., that the language/world hookup is arbitrary), it follows that human subjects cannot accurately represent the world only if we grant the further erroneous claim that representational entities are limited to language (and certain sensations). But this is precisely what the sophisticated correspondence theorist denies.

Again, Richard Rorty says, "To say that truth is not out there is simply to say that where there are no sentences there is not truth, that sentences are elements of human language, and that human languages are human creations. Truth cannot be out

there—cannot exist independently of the human mind—because
sentences cannot so exist, or be out there. . . . Only descriptions
. . . can be true and false."[10] It should be obvious that Rorty
attacks a straw man and that his argument goes through only if
we grant that sentences are the fundamental truth-bearers.

5. *Confusions about perception and intentionality.*
Postmodernists adopt a highly contentious model of perception
and intentionality, often without argument, and they seem to
enjoin serious consideration of a prima facie, more plausible
model. The result is that postmodernists are far too pessimistic
about the prospects of human epistemic success.

Postmodernists adopt a linguistic version of René
Descartes's idea theory of perception (and intentionality generally). To understand the idea theory, and the postmodern adap-
tation of it, a good place to start is with a commonsense, critical
realist view of perception. According to critical realism, when a
subject is looking at a red object such as an apple, the object
itself is the direct object of the sensory state. What one sees
directly is the apple itself. True, one must have a sensation of red
to apprehend the apple, but on the critical realist view, the sensation of red is to be understood as a case of being-appeared-to-
redly and analyzed as a self-presenting property. What is a
self-presenting property? If property F is a self-presenting one,
then it is by means of F that a relevant external object is presented directly to a person, and F presents itself directly to the
person as well. Thus, F presents its object mediately though
directly, and itself immediately.

This is not as hard to understand as it first may appear.
Sensations, such as being-appeared-to-redly, are an important
class of self-presenting properties. If Jones is having a sensation
of red while looking at an apple, then having the property of
being-appeared-to-redly as part of his consciousness modifies his
substantial self. When Jones has this sensation, it is a tool that

presents the red apple mediately to him, and the sensation also presents itself to Jones. What does it mean to say that the sensation presents the apple to him mediately? Simply this: it is in virtue of or by means of the sensation that Jones directly sees the apple itself.

Moreover, by having the sensation of red, Jones is directly aware both of the apple and of his own awareness of the apple. For the critical realist, the sensation of red may, indeed, be a tool or means that Jones uses to become aware of the apple, but he is thereby directly aware of the apple. His awareness of the apple is direct in that nothing stands between Jones and the apple, not even his sensation of the apple. That sensation presents the apple directly, though as a tool Jones must have the sensation as a necessary condition for seeing the apple. On the critical realist view, a knowing subject is not trapped behind or within anything, including a viewpoint, a narrative, a historical-linguistic perspective. To have an entity in the external world as an object of intentionality is to already be "out there"; there is no need to escape anything. One is not trapped behind one's eyeballs or anything else. It is a basic fallacy of logic to infer that one sees a point-of-viewed-object from the fact that one sees an object from a point of view.

Before leaving the critical realist view, it is important to say that the theory does not limit self-presenting properties to those associated with the five senses and, therefore, does not limit the objects of direct awareness to ordinary sensory objects. The critical realist will say that a knowing subject is capable of direct acquaintance with a host of non-sense-perceptible objects—one's own ego and its mental states, various abstract objects like the laws of mathematics or logic, and spirit beings, including God.

By contrast, for Descartes's idea theory, one's ideas—in this case, sensations—stand between the subject and the object of perception. Jones is directly aware of his own sensation of the apple and indirectly aware of the apple in the sense that it is what causes the sensation to happen. On the idea theory, a perceiving subject is trapped behind his own sensations and cannot get outside them to the external world in order to compare his sensations to their objects to see if those sensations are accurate.

Now, in a certain sense, postmodernists believe that people are trapped behind something in the attempt to get to the external world. However, for them the wall between people and reality is not composed of sensations as it was for Descartes; rather, it is constituted by one's community and its linguistic categories and practices. One's language serves as a sort of distorting and, indeed, creative filter. One cannot get outside one's language to see if one's talk about the world is the way the world is. Thus, Grenz advocates a new outlook, allegedly representing some sort of consensus in the human sciences, that expresses "a more profound understanding of epistemology. Recent thinking has helped us see that the process of knowing, and to some extent even the process of experiencing the world, can occur only within a conceptual framework, a framework mediated by the social community in which we participate."[11]

It has been noted repeatedly that such assertions are self-refuting. For if we are all trapped behind a framework such that simple, direct seeing is impossible, then no amount of recent thinking can help us see anything; all it could do would be to invite us to see something as such and such from within a conceptual framework. Given the self-refuting nature of such claims, and given the fact that we all experience regularly the activity of comparing our conceptions of an entity with the entity itself as a way of adjusting those conceptions, it is hard to see why anyone, especially a Christian, would adopt the postmodern view. In any case, I have seldom seen the realist perspective seriously considered by postmodern thinkers, and until it is, statements like Grenz's will be taken as mere mantras by many of us.

V. FINAL REMARKS ABOUT THE IMMORAL NATURE OF POSTMODERNISM

For some time I have been convinced that postmodernism is rooted in pervasive confusions, and I have tried to point out what some of these are. I am also convinced that postmodernism is an irresponsible, cowardly abrogation of the duties that constitute a disciple's calling to be a Christian intellectual and teacher.

In her provocative book entitled *Longing to Know*, Esther Meek asserts that humans as knowers exercise a profound responsibility to submit to the authoritative dictates of reality.[12] Thus, "It is not responsible to deny objective truth and reality in knowing; it is irresponsible. It is not responsible to make the human knower or community of knowers the arbiters of a private truth and reality; it is irresponsible."[13] Again, Meek claims that "[g]ood, responsible knowing brings blessing, shalom; irresponsible knowing brings curse."[14] In another place Meek warns that "the kind of freedom implied by the thought that we humans completely determine our reality leaves us with a gnawing sense of the relative insignificance of our choices. I think it leads not to total responsibility but to careless irresponsibility, both with regard to ourselves and with regard to other humans, not to mention to the world. And, paradoxically, it leads not to a deeper sense of [communal or individual] identity and dignity but to a disheartening lack of it."[15]

We evangelicals need to pay careful attention to Meek's claims. As humans, we live and ought to live our lives not merely by truth but by knowledge of truth. Knowledge of truth gives us confident trust and access to reality. Moreover, as those called to be teachers and scholars for the church and, indeed, for the unbelieving world, we are called not only to impart and defend truth, but to impart and defend knowledge of truth and, even more, to impart and defend knowledge of truth as knowledge of truth. This entails that we must impart and defend the notion that we do, in fact, have knowledge of important spiritual and ethical truths. Among other things, this gives confidence in truth and knowledge to those we serve. Thus, we are irresponsible not simply if we fail to achieve knowledge of reality; we are doubly irresponsible if we fail to impart to others knowledge as knowledge. The corrosive effects of postmodernism eat away at the fulfillment of these duties and responsibilities that constitute our calling from Almighty God.

Meek goes on to point out that the achieving of knowledge and the teaching of it as knowledge "calls for courageous resolve. And this courageous resolve, when proven true, merits the deep admiration of others."[16] The need for such courage is especially grave today as we labor in an intellectual milieu in which the worldviews of naturalism and postmodernism both entail that there is no non-empirical knowledge, especially no religious or ethical knowledge.

Faced with such opposition and the pressure it brings, postmodernism is a form of intellectual pacifism that, at the end of the day, recommends backgammon while the barbarians are at the gate. It is the easy, cowardly way out that removes the pressure to engage alternative conceptual schemes, to be different, to risk ridicule, to take a stand outside the gate. But it is precisely as disciples of Christ, even more, as officers in his army, that the pacifist way out is simply not an option. However comforting it may be, postmodernism is the cure that kills the patient, the military strategy that concedes defeat before the first shot is fired, the ideology that undermines its own claims to allegiance. And it is an immoral, coward's way out that is not worthy of a movement born out of the martyrs' blood.[17]

4

LOST IN INTERPRETATION? TRUTH, SCRIPTURE, AND HERMENEUTICS[1]

Kevin J. Vanhoozer

Kevin J. Vanhoozer, research professor of systematic theology at Trinity Evangelical Divinity School, Deerfield, Illinois, delivered this plenary address at the 56th annual meeting of the Evangelical Theological Society on November 19, 2004, in San Antonio, Texas.

I. INTRODUCTION: STORIES OF TRUTH AND INTERPRETATION

Biblical interpretation is the soul of theology. Truth is the ultimate accolade that we accord an interpretation. Christian theology therefore succeeds or fails in direct proportion to its ability to render true interpretations of the word of God written.

They asked for a plenary paper on truth and interpretation. It took me some time to figure out what they meant. Only when I put it in canonical context—the ETS program book!—did I realize that I had to discuss the use of the Bible in theology, because systematic theology was not otherwise represented as such in the other plenaries. My focus is thus on doctrine, the main product of theology's interpretation of Scripture, and hence the linchpin between biblical interpretation and theological truth.

1. *Pilgrim's egress: setting out.* There has been too much wrangling over whether evangelicalism is a matter of doctrine or piety, the head or the heart. Those who see the essence of evangelicalism in pietistic terms tend to see the Bible primarily as a means of spiritual sustenance. Those who see the essence of evangelicalism in doctrinal terms tend to see the Bible primarily as a means of propositional communication. It is neither necessary nor advisable to take sides in this debate.[2] Indeed, to do so is to reduce, and so distort, the very concept of biblical and doctrinal truth. Let no one put asunder what God has joined together. Far better to see the Christian life as a way where head and heart come together to get the feet moving. We evangelicals need to put feet on the gospel, and on our doctrine. Evangelical theology should provide direction for walking the way of truth and life.

John Bunyan knew this long ago. His *Pilgrim's Progress* pictures Christian as a wayfarer directed by a Book on a way to the City of God. Christian's neighbor, Pliable, asks him if the words of his Book are certainly true. "Yes verily," Christian replies, "for it was made by him that cannot lie." Evangelist then leads Christian to the Wicket Gate where, he says, he will "receive instruction [doctrine] about the way." In Bunyan's words, "[Evangelist] told him that after he was gone some distance from the gate, he would come to the House of the Interpreter, at whose door he should knock; and he would show him excellent things."

2. *Why are they saying such awful things about truth and interpretation?* Fast forward to the twentieth century: "All this stuff about hermeneutics is really a way of avoiding the truth

question." So spoke homo Tyndaliens, Tyndale man, to be precise, a New Testament Ph.D. student at Tyndale House, Cambridge, in 1984. My immediate reply: no, all this stuff about truth is really a way of avoiding the hermeneutical question. What I now want to say to my erstwhile colleague is this: all this stuff about hermeneutics is a way of facing up to the truth question: "Hermeneutics has become a bogey with which to frighten the children, and yet . . . its message is really rather simple. Appropriating ancient . . . texts [and not ancient only!] requires an effort of understanding and not just philological skills."[3]

Contemporary evangelicals had best face up to both questions. The temptation of conservative evangelicals is to play the propositional truth card in order to trump interpretation; the temptation of what we might call "emergent" evangelicals is to play the interpretation card in order to trump propositional truth. Neither move is ultimately satisfying, nor edifying.[4]

3. *"Lost in interpretation": how hermeneutics complicates "Bible and theology."* In what sense are we "lost in interpretation"? I mean (at least) four things by this phrase (apologies to Walt Kaiser and other single-sense folk!).

a. *The author is lost in interpretation.* There is a tendency in certain contemporary approaches to interpretation to lose the author, either because the author is historically distant or because the author has drowned in the sea of linguistic indeterminacy. This lostness is a loss, a death, and with the death of the author goes what may be the last best hope for a criterion of validity.[5]

b. *The subject matter is lost in interpretation.* "Lost in interpretation" also means lost in translation: something of the text's subject matter fails to get through. Some forms of historical criticism lose the theological substance of the Scriptures. Some forms of literary criticism lose the history of Israel.[6]

c. *Truth is lost in interpretation.* Third, in the context of philosophical hermeneutics, the truth itself is often lost in interpretation. Gianni Vattimo notes that hermeneutics has "become a sort of *koinē* or common idiom of Western culture."[7] He further observes that the notion of interpretation has become so broad in the work of philosophers like Gadamer and Ricoeur that it virtually coincides with every kind of human experience of the world: "That each experience of truth is an experience of interpretation is almost a truism in today's culture."[8] Truth is lost when there are no facts, only historically located interpretations.[9]

d. *The interpreter is lost in interpretation*. The last thing lost in interpretation is the reader. The Ethiopian eunuch was lost in interpretation. "Do you understand what you are reading?" Philip asks. "How can I, unless someone guides me?" (Acts 8:31). To be lost in interpretation is to know neither the "where" nor the "way." Having the right methods takes us only so far; biblical interpretation is less a matter of calculus than it is of good judgment. The most intractable problems of interpretation are a function not of semantics but of spiritual direction. I have therefore decided that the genre of a plenary paper is as much pastoral as it is professional. Better: it is a pastoral word to theological professionals. To the hermeneutically complacent, I bring a word of challenge; to the hermeneutically distressed, I bring a word of consolation. But we begin by clarifying the current situation.

II. TRUTH AND INTERPRETATION: THE CURRENT SITUATION

1. *"You are here": postmodernity and the situated interpreter*. In our garden we have a stepping stone that reads: "You are here." But where, pray tell, is "here"? We are in a crisis situation, in a labyrinth of language, at the crossroads of truth and interpretation. To paraphrase Barth: as Christian theologians, we must speak of truth; as denizens of the twenty-first century, post-Enlightenment west, we cannot speak of truth.

Context is vital for establishing textual meaning. This much is well known, and agreed on. Yet today the context or location of the reader has become more significant for biblical interpretation than the context of the author. In the 1950s, Bultmann asked whether exegesis without presuppositions was possible. By the 1980s, we were being told that it was impossible for exegetes to transcend their ideological locations. Postmodernity is the triumph of situatedness—in race, gender, class—over detached objectivity.

Some follow Nietzsche and conclude that there are no facts, that it is interpretation all the way down. Never mind the balm, is there no bedrock in Gilead? Postmoderns typically think of interpretation as a political act, a means of colonizing and capturing texts and whole fields of discourse. Where have we come to? I knew where I was—in trouble!—when my doctoral students at Edinburgh University accused me of oppressing them with my truth claims (no charges were filed). There is some truth in the observation that raw power often appears as an angel of truth. What postmodernity teaches is ultimately a negative lesson, one moreover that we should have already learned from the biblical prophets—namely, that we are situated, limited, contingent, and have a disposition toward idolatry. While God's word is infallible, human interpretations are not. God is in heaven; we are on earth. Situated between heaven and earth, we lack the knowledge of angels.

What, then, are our options? (1) Hermeneutical relativism: embrace the interpreter within you and live as they did in the period of the Judges where everyone did what was right in their own eyes (so long as you don't hurt anyone, presumably!); (2) take the road to Rome and the safety of numbers; (3) join an independent church, where right reading is a function of one's local interpretive community. None of these options inspires confidence. I propose a fourth possibility: that we set out like pilgrims on the way indicated by our Book, that we employ whatever hermeneutical tools available that help us follow its sense, that we pray for the illumination of the Spirit and for the humility to acknowledge our missteps, and that we consult other pilgrims who have gone before us as well as Christians in other parts of today's world.

What we must not do is postpone setting out until we have resolved all interpretative questions. What we see practiced all too often in the academy is a "hermeneutics of procrastination"—"always reading and never coming to a knowledge of the truth" (to slightly paraphrase 2 Tim. 3:7), and never walking truth's way. This is what Derrida implies when he speaks of meaning "endlessly deferred." Kierkegaard was well-acquainted with this phenomenon, and he saw it for what it was: a spiritual rather than an intellectual condition. Imagine a country in which a king issues a decree and his subjects set out to interpret rather than respond to it. "Everything is interpretation—but no one reads the royal ordinance in such a way that he acts accordingly."[10] Ours too is a "culture of interpretation" where the business of interpretation is busyness. The hermeneutics of procrastination is motored up, but the motor is not in gear, only idling. The solution? A "hermeneutics of activation" that engages the matter of the text. But how?

2. *Truth and other interpretative interests: postmodernity and the next Reformation?* Some in our midst believe that we should embrace our new cultural and intellectual situation. Carl Raschke has recently argued that postmodernity provides an opportunity for evangelicals to reclaim their Reformation heritage, especially the notions of *sola fide* and *sola scriptura*.[11] Raschke and other "emerging" evangelicals contend that their conservative counterparts have co-opted the notion of biblical truth to modern theories of language and knowledge—in a word, to secular philosophy. The notion of objective truth leaves these interpreters cold: "The strictly theoretical seems inert."[12]

Far better to read in order to meet people's needs, promote justice, and transform the world. (It was Marx who said that the point is not to interpret the world, but to change it. Pity an evangelical didn't say that!)

Far better still, say emerging evangelicals, to enter into a personal relation with God characterized more by trust than by reason. The interest that governs emerging evangelicals' biblical interpretation is salvation—not doctrinal formulation, not system-building. Note well: Raschke does not pit postmodernity against truth (he lays relativism and skepticism on the doorstep of modernity). On the contrary, postmodernity is at its root an insight into language that privileges its vocative rather than descriptive function. With Levinas, Raschke views the word not as a sign that indicates a thing but as a call from an other. Emerging evangelicals posit the priority of relations (interlocutions) over predications (locutions), the priority of personal over propositional reality.[13] "Truth and interpretation" in the context of emergent evangelicalism is about faces, not facts.

People read the Bible today, then, with a wide variety of interpretive interests—saintly, scholarly, and otherwise. Some have an interest in the state of the Hebrew or Greek language at the time a particular text was written or in filling out the historical background of the text; others have an interest in the text's literary structure, in chiasms, or the way it achieves its rhetorical effects; still others have an interest in the way a text expresses a particular understanding of human existence, or in the way a text envisions women, or in the effect a text may have on matters of social justice. These are all legitimate interests, to be sure. But how should one interpret Scripture if one's primary interest is in the text's theological truth? More pointedly: is the truth of Scripture personal/relational or propositional/doctrinal? The future of evangelical theology may well depend on how it answers this question.[14]

III. TRUTH AND INTERPRETATION: THE STANDARD PICTURE

1. *"Mining the deposit of truth": The Hodge-Henry hypothesis.* For large swaths of the Western tradition, the task of theology consisted in mining propositional nuggets from the biblical deposit of truth. The Pauline shaft in particular was thought to contain several rich doctrinal lodes.

a. *Thomas Aquinas.* According to Thomas Aquinas, Scripture contains the science of God: the unified teaching from God about God. The operative term is teaching. Doctrine is essentially sacred teaching, a divinely revealed informative proposition about an objective reality.[15] In the words of one commentator, revelation for Aquinas "is an intellectual event": a communication from the mind of God to human minds.[16] Theology is a theoretical and practical science that infers the truth of things by considering them in the light of the sacred teaching contained in Scripture.[17]

b. *Charles Hodge.* In a different context, nineteenth-century Princeton, Charles Hodge and B. B. Warfield laid the groundwork for conservative evangelical theology by insisting on the importance of propositional truth, not least as a counter to Schleiermacher's liberalism, in which doctrine is merely religious feeling set forth in speech.[18] As with Aquinas, the Bible is the deposit of revealed truth. The manner in which theology is a "science" of Scripture, however, is noticeably different. Hodge bases his understanding on the inductive method that dominated the natural sciences of his day. The Bible contains revealed data, not only soteric data (e.g., gospel truths of salvation), but scientific, historical, and geographic data as well, not only because these too are the words of God, but also because the gospel is inextricably intertwined with real events in the world. Everything thus depends on getting the Bible right through a process of empirical observation and logical deduction: "The

Bible is to the theologian what nature is to the man of science.
It is his storehouse of facts."[19] The theologian's duty is to ascer-
tain, collect, and combine the biblical facts.

   c. *Carl F. H. Henry.* Carl F. H. Henry's magisterial defense
of propositional revelation follows in the same tradition. He
defines a proposition as "a verbal statement that is either true
or false."[20] The Scriptures, says Henry, contain a divinely given
body of information actually expressed or capable of being
expressed in propositions. Those parts of the Bible that are not
already in the form of statements may be paraphrased in propositional form.[21] In Henry's words: "Christian theology is the sys-
tematization of the truth-content explicit and implicit in the
inspired writings."[22]

   In what we may call the Hodge-Henry (H-H) hypothesis,
doctrine is the result of biblical induction and deduction, a cap-
sule summary of the meaning of Scripture "taken as a set of
propositional statements, each expressing a divine affirmation,
valid always and everywhere."[23] Propositionalist theology tends
to see Scripture in terms of revelation, revelation in terms of conveying information, and theology in terms of divine informa-
tion-processing.

   2. *Correspondence as a picturing relation.* The H-H hypothesis is heavily invested in a particular theory of language, meaning, and truth. Language according to the H-H hypothesis is
primarily concerned with stating truth, which in turn is a function of describing reality, representing the world, or recording a
series of events. Meaning here becomes largely a matter of
ostensive reference, a matter of indicating objects or states of
affairs. The biblical text is a mirror of nature, history, and even
eternity to the extent that it can state universal truths about
God's being. Moreover, Scripture is not like those fun house mirrors that distort reality, enlarging heads in grotesque fashion or
(which is better) making the stout appear thin. Rather, the bib-

lical text pictures reality as it really is. Hence "truth" is a correspondence relation in which language (and thought) accurately reflects, mirrors, or pictures reality. It is worth noting that this concept of truth lives off a visual metaphor: to "see" with the mind's eye is to obtain theoretical truth (*theoria* = "to behold").[24]

Emergent evangelicals are not the only ones who wonder whether this theory of language, meaning, and truth owes more to philosophy than to the Bible.[25] Raschke, for example, charges conservative evangelicals with shoring up their commitment to biblical authority with a metaphysical theory of truth that is neither biblical in its origin nor plausible in the contemporary context. He rejects the notion that theology is best conceived in terms of subjects (theologians) "seeing" objects (biblical propositions).[26] Postmoderns no longer believe in the innocent eye, even—nay, especially!—when it is the mind's eye.

The H-H hypothesis bears a certain resemblance to the early Wittgenstein's "picture theory" of the proposition where words refer to objects and sentences refer to empirical facts.[27] Words and propositions are the atoms and molecules of a language that is mainly pictorial. But texts are not simply bundles of propositions, but new kinds of entities altogether with new emergent properties. Just as one cannot account for everything in a biological organism with the categories of physics and chemistry, so one cannot account for everything in a text at the level of what we might call "molecular hermeneutics." The main problem with the picture theory, then, is that it seems singularly inadequate to explain *textual* meaning.

There are further problems with the picture theory of meaning and truth. First, and most importantly, it fails sufficiently to recognize that we use language to do other things beside referring. And it is far from clear that all reference to the real is best thought of as "picturing." Second, and relatedly, it ignores the

role of circumstances, context, and use for determining meaning (e.g., what we are doing with language). According to David
Clark, a proposition is an abstraction that captures the informative content of a statement but strips away "all the dimensions of the statement that do something other than tell how
things are."[28] And, third, in seeking propositional restatements
of Scripture it implies that there is something inadequate about
the Bible's own forms of language and literature. The early
Wittgenstein makes a similar complaint about ordinary language: "Language disguises thought. So much so, that from the
outward form of the clothing it is impossible to infer the form
of the thought beneath it."[29] Evangelicals should resist the implication that there is something improper about the final form of
Scripture.[30] Is there not a better way to conceive of the relation
of meaning and truth?

3. *Is inerrancy a hermeneutic?* The moral thus far is: views
of meaning and truth have serious consequences for the way theologians handle Scripture. Carl Henry was right to worry that
some theories of interpretation serve to "neutralize" inerrancy.[31]
This leads naturally to our next question: is inerrancy itself a
hermeneutic? Our preliminary response must be, "Yes and no."
Positively, inerrancy assumes the ultimate unity of the Bible, a
crucial hermeneutical premise. On the other hand, simply to
assume the Bible's truth is not yet to say what it means. Even
Paul Tillich could affirm that the Bible's message was "grounded
in reality," since for him its message concerns the Ground of our
Being! Fully to do justice to the topic of truth and interpretation,
then, requires us to do two things: to understand what inerrancy
means and to understand what it means in particular for biblical interpretation.

a. *Inerrancy and the bearers of truth.* At this point it would
be helpful to distinguish the truth of the text from our interpretations of it. Believe it or not, another Cambridge doctoral stu-

dent once asked me, "Aren't our evangelical interpretations inerrant?" Perhaps I lead a sheltered life, but I found, and continue to find, this sentiment shocking. If nothing else, it has helped me clarify a distinction between different bearers of truth. We need to distinguish the text as a truth-bearer from the interpretation (or the interpreter) as a truth-bearer. The Bible's witness to its subject matter is always true; the interpreter's witness to the text, by contrast, suffers from various forms of existential short-sightedness, confessional tunnel vision, and cultural myopia. Yet the vocation of the interpreter is to be nothing less than a witness to the truth of the text and hence to the subject matter that it attests.

b. *Inerrancy as underdetermined hermeneutic.* Back to our question: is inerrancy a theory of interpretation? As we have seen, the assumption that the Bible exhibits a unified truth, while a vital hermeneutical presupposition, nevertheless underdetermines the exegetical results. Just as inspiration does not tell us what the Bible means or how it functions as an authority in theology (this was the moral of David Kelsey's *Proving Doctrine: The Uses of Scripture in Modern Theology*[32]), so inerrancy—the belief that the Bible speaks truly in all that it affirms—does not necessarily generate interpretative agreement even among those who hold to it.

Truth may be the correspondence of "what one says" to "what is," but it falls to interpretation to discern what it is that the biblical authors are affirming, and whether there is more than one way of saying something about it: "The issue . . . is not whether Scripture is 'inerrant' nor certainly whether the God who speaks therein is 'inerrant,' but the nature of the Scripture that the inerrant God has given us."[33] It is one thing to posit the Bible's truthfulness in all that it affirms, quite another to say what the truth of the Bible is. Inerrancy alone, then, is not yet a full-fledged hermeneutic. For many church fathers, the entire truthfulness of Scripture was compatible with allegorizing. Contemporary evangelicals, by contrast, are more likely to equate truthfulness with historicity.

c. *Inerrancy in Chicago: "Just the facts, ma'am."* Well, why not? Why not stick with the "facts"? Because critics of propositionalist theology charge it with selling out to modernity (and to secular philosophy) by assuming that biblical meaning and truth are functions of historical reference and empirical actuality. Raschke argues that the traditional notion of infallibility "was never intended to guarantee a precise, literal 'factual' truth of every single biblical sentence."[34] Is inerrancy really the illegitimate child of evangelical faith and modernity? And has a modern distortion or reduction of truth proved inimical to evangelical theological interpretation?

In this regard it is interesting to compare the two Chicago Statements. The Statement on Biblical Inerrancy is in my opinion by far the more successful of the two. Interestingly, one looks in vain in that statement for the terms "fact" or "factuality." The Statement speaks instead of the truth of Scripture in "all matters" it addresses (Art. IX, XI). The Statement acknowledges the presence of diverse literary styles (Art. VIII, XVIII) and figures of speech: "So history must be treated as history, poetry as poetry, hyperbole and metaphor as hyperbole and metaphor . . . and so forth." The key claim for our purposes comes in Article XIII: "We deny that it is proper to evaluate Scripture according to standards of truth and error that are alien to its usage or purpose."

In contrast, the second Chicago Statement, on Biblical Hermeneutics, takes back with its left hand what the former offers with its right. On the one hand, Article X affirms "that Scripture communicates God's truth to us verbally through a wide variety of literary forms." And Article XV helpfully adds that "[i]nterpretation according to the literal sense will take account of all figures of speech and literary forms found in the text." These gestures are overwhelmed by other articles, however, where the language of "fact" and "factuality" takes over. Article VI: "We . . . affirm that a statement is true if it represents matters as they actually are but is an error if it misrepresents the facts."[35] Article XIV goes on to affirm that the biblical record of events, "though presented in a variety of appropriate literary forms, corresponds to historical fact." Finally, Article XXII affirms that Genesis 1—11 "is factual, as is the rest of the book." It is difficult to read these affirmations together so as to preserve a healthy tension rather than a contradiction between them. While the second Statement does not actually make shipwreck of biblical interpretation, it does incline the good ship Hermeneutics to list rather dangerously.

Dangerously? Yes, to the extent that it risks imposing extrabiblical categories and standards on biblical narratives. History is not simply a matter of reporting facts, at least not if by "fact" we mean the kind of data that can be verified empirically apart from a fiduciary interpretative framework! That way positivism lies.[36] Evangelicals must not let a particular theory of truth and factuality determine what the author of Genesis 1—11 is proposing for our consideration. It is the text, not some theory of truth, that ought to determine what kind of a claim is being made. To begin with a theory of truth and argue to a particular interpretation is to put the factual cart before the hermeneutical horse. This was Bultmann's mistake: he assumed that the Bible's truth was existential and then set about demythologizing it. Let us not make a similar mistake and run roughshod over authorial intent in our haste to historicize.

IV. TRUTH AND INTERPRETATION: A PROPOSAL

1. *Gospel and truth: beyond "cheap inerrancy."*
   a. *Will the real people of the book stand up?* Today the sta-

tus of evangelicals as "people of the book" is in jeopardy, and
perhaps not without reason. In the good old days, the dividing
lines were clearly drawn: the liberals revised the faith in light of
modern learning and culture, while conservative evangelicals
stood guard over the deposit of truth. Then a stranger came to
town and stood up to the theological outlaws. It was high noon
on modernity, and Karl Barth was riding again, this time with a
postliberal posse. It is sobering to reflect that it was second-gen-
eration Barthians like Hans Frei and George Lindbeck, not
evangelicals, who were largely responsible for the demise of lib-
eral theology and for the rehabilitation of "biblical" as a
respectable theological label. Of course, the crucial question—
and not only for our topic of truth and interpretation—continues to be, "What does it mean to be biblical?"

In the big geotheopolitical picture, postliberals and evangelicals are allies: postliberals are generously orthodox, trinitarian, and Christocentric. But they are not so sure about us.
Hans Frei, for example, worries that Carl Henry is a closet modernist because of his commitment to truth as historical factuality. For Frei, it is the biblical narrative itself, not its propositional
paraphrase, that is the truth-bearer. Whereas for Henry doctrines state the meaning of the narratives, for Frei we only
understand the doctrine by understanding the story.[37] Emergent
evangelicals have similar questions about their conservative
counterparts. Raschke, for example, says, "Inerrantism
amounts to the rehellenizing of the faith and a retreat from the
Reformation."[38]

Conservative evangelicals are not the only people of the
book, nor the only people of the gospel. Other theological traditions too profess the truth of Jesus Christ. The issue, then, is
twofold: what kind of truth does Scripture have, and how does
it speak truth? Each of these questions has a bearing on the
nature and purpose of Christian doctrine.

Carl Henry was absolutely right to stress the cognitive content of Scripture and doctrine over against those who sought to make revelation a noncognitive experience. Is it possible, however, that in so focusing on biblical content he, and other conservative evangelicals, have overlooked the significance of biblical literary form? We shall return to this point below. The immediate point is this: of all theological traditions, evangelicals must respect the nature of the biblical books they interpret. It is no service to the Bible to make a literary-category mistake. At least on this point, I agree with James Barr: "Genre mistakes cause the wrong kind of truth values to be attached to the biblical sentences."[39] The dialogue between conservative and emergent evangelicals could be helped by a recognition of the cognitive significance of Scripture's literary forms.

To interpret the Bible truly, then, we must do more than string together individual propositions like beads on a string. This takes us only as far as fortune cookie theology, to a practice of breaking open Scripture in order to find the message contained within. What gets lost in propositionalist interpretation are the circumstances of the statement, its poetic and affective elements, and even, then, a dimension of its truth. We do less than justice to Scripture if we preach and teach only its propositional content. Information alone is insufficient for spiritual formation. We need to get beyond "cheap inerrancy," beyond ascribing accolades to the Bible to understanding what the Bible is actually saying, beyond professing biblical truth to practicing it.

b. *"The gospel according to . . .": an evangelical definition of truth.* How can we understand the Bible according to a standard of truth that is not foreign to its purpose? Here we do well to recall C. S. Lewis's distinction: "truth is always about something; but reality is that about which truth is."[40] So what is the Bible about regarding eternal truths, historical facts, morals,

God, us? There are repeated textual clues. Take, for instance, this title: "The gospel according to . . ." The Bible is more than a system of philosophy or moral truths. It is good news. The instinct of cognitive-propositional theology is sound. The gospel is informative: "he is risen." Without some propositional core, the church would lose its raison d'être, leaving only programs and potlucks. At the same time, to reduce the truth of Scripture to a set of propositions is unnecessarily reductionist. What the Bible as a whole is literally about is theodrama—the words and deeds of God on the stage of world history that climax in Jesus Christ.

"The gospel according to Matthew" (or Mark, Luke, or John). To speak of the evangel is to focus on the truth of the subject matter of this apostolic discourse; to mention the evangelists is to focus on the truth of authorial discourse. It is not insignificant that most books in the Bible bear the names of their reputed authors. This is because the Bible is largely testimony: someone saying something to someone about what one has seen and heard. To affirm the truth of the gospel ("He is risen") is to view truth as the correspondence between the author's discourse (not the words taken out of context!) and the way things are.[41]

c. *The orthodox gospel: a catholic criterion of truth.* Affirming truth as correspondence ("truth is always about something") takes us only so far. We still have to determine what the Bible means ("that about which truth is"). The ancient Rule of Faith specifies what the Bible's truth is ultimately about: the creative and redemptive work of the triune God. To counter heretical interpretations that fundamentally mistook "that about which the gospel is," Irenaeus and Tertullian put forward the Rule of Faith as the necessary interpretative framework for understanding Scripture correctly. Inasmuch as it specifies what the Bible is about and how it is unified, the Rule of Faith serves as a crucial principle for true interpretation.

Theology should be catholic, not in the Roman sense of according magisterial authority to the official tradition of the institutional church, but rather in recognizing what we might call the ministerial authority of the consensus tradition of the church as it is extended through time and space. Catholicity is the antidote to the tribalism and parochialism that infects Christian thinking that never leaves its ghetto. When each inter-preter lives in his own house, the result is a destructive faction-alism ("I am of Piper"; "I am of Dobson"; "I am of McClaren").

2. *Truth as theodramatic correspondence: doctrine and the unity of divine action.* To interpret the Bible we need to do more than grasp a few isolated truths; we need to be able to grasp the whole, and to situate the parts in the whole. The unity of the Bible is neither that of a philosophical system nor a system of moral truths. On the contrary, the unified sum and substance of the Bible is theodramatic: it is all about God's word and God's deeds, accomplished by his "two hands" (Son and Spirit) and about what we should say and do in response. It is because the-ology's subject matter is theodramatic that it must do more with the Bible (the script) than squeeze out its propositional truth. The Bible is not just our authoritative script; it is one of the lead-ing players in the ongoing drama, interrupting our complacency, demanding its reader's response. The biblical texts were not written merely "to be objects of aesthetic beauty or contempla-tion, but as persuasive forces that during their own time formed opinion, made judgments, and exerted change."[42] To focus on propositional content only is to fail to recognize the Bible as divine communicative action, a failure that leads one to dedra-matize the Scriptures. The result: a faith that seeks only an abbreviated understanding that falls short of performance knowledge.[43]

Doctrine is an aid to faith's search for understanding. In the first place, doctrine helps us understand what God has done in

Jesus Christ. This is the indicative, "already" aspect of doctrinal truth. Yet there is a second, imperatival aspect of doctrine that directs us to demonstrate our understanding by joining in the action. What God is doing in Christ is not simply something past but ongoing. Genuinely to understand the theodrama, then, means participating in it now. To become a Christian is not to become a subscriber to a philosophy; it is to become an active participant in God's triune mission to the world, following Jesus in the power of the Spirit to speak and act in ways that fit the new created order "in Christ." This is the imperatival dimension of doctrine: do the truth; become what you are. Doctrine, then, is theodramatic instruction; or to continue the theatrical metaphor, doctrine is direction for our fitting participation in the drama of redemption.

Doctrinal truth thus becomes a matter of theodramatic correspondence between our words and deeds and God's words and deeds. Theodramatic correspondence means life and language that is in accord with the gospel and according to the Scriptures. We speak and do the truth when our words and actions display theodramatic "fittingness."

Theodramatic correspondence yields an "enlarged" sense of truth and interpretation alike. Doctrine is "according to" the Scriptures when it displays, as my dictionary puts it, "harmonious correspondence," a rich agreement of pitch, tone, and color. And it does so without leaving the proposition behind. It is crucial not to miss this point. I have come neither to praise nor to bury the proposition but to incorporate it into a larger model of truth and interpretation. I regret that the proposition has become despised and rejected by theologians. I affirm that there is propositional revelation in the Bible. But I also believe that there is more than propositional revelation that demands our attention as theologians. God is a dialogical agent who uses propositions to perform many kinds of speech acts—commanding, promising, and yes, asserting—speech acts that are just as much concerned with establishing covenantal relations as they are with conveying information.

Note that it is just as big a mistake to treat all the Bible as narrative as it is to reduce it all to propositions. Here, too, the paradigm of drama proves helpful, for many kinds of communicative acts coexist within a single play. A play may include moments of recitative, where narrative predominates, as well as aria-like passages where song and poetry may come to the fore. And let's not forget how dialogue structures many biblical books; both Job and John actually resemble playscripts.[44]

3. *Truth as cartographic correspondence: doctrine and the plurality of testimony.* The notion of correspondence stems more from an intuition— not least, an intuition about what a confession of the gospel requires for it really to be good news— than a fully worked out theory. Aristotle says that truth is what you get when you say of "what is that it is." I think Aristotle's intuition is sound. We have seen that the content of evangelical truth, what it is about, is theodramatic. Yet Aristotle's intuition does not help with the inevitable follow-up question: how does one say "that it is"? Is there only one right way to say "that it is," or may we say of truth what Aristotle himself says of Being, namely, that it may be said in many ways?

I have already mentioned the drawbacks of the mirroring or picture theory of correspondence. The map of the Paris métro corresponds to the Paris métro, but not as a picture or mirror corresponds. For one thing, the "language" of the map is not representational; the tracks in the métro are not actually purple, red, and orange! Nevertheless, I believe the metaphor of the map can help us chart a way forward with regard to truth and interpretation. While "script" captures the theodramatic unity of Scripture, "atlas" catches the irreducible plurality of Scripture, the many ways the theodrama is rendered. The Bible is a literary atlas: a collection of book-maps that variously render the way, the truth, and the life. Note that both "script" and "map" are texts that provide directions. And this is the ultimate purpose of Scripture: to direct us to Christ, the way of truth and life.

Truth is the fit between text and reality, between what is written and what is written about. But maps remind us that there is more than one kind of fit. We can map the same terrain according to a variety of different keys and scales. A road map need not contradict a map that highlights topography, or a map that highlights historical landmarks and points of scenic interest, or a plat of survey that shows where properties begin and end. Each type of map reflects a certain interest.

Propositionalist theology, by contrast, risks reading Scripture as if one size fits all, as it were, or rather, as if there were only one kind of fit. Yet the Spirit has not seen fit to inspire one kind of text only. We need, therefore, to acknowledge "breathing space" as it were between the biblical discourse and the subject matter of that discourse.[45] When we do, we will see that there is more than one way to "map" reality. The proof is: there is no such thing as a universal, all-purpose map. A map is actually an interpretative framework, not a mirror of nature. Maps highlight what they want their readers to know. Some maps tell you about the borders of various countries; others tell you where to find buried treasure.

It is one thing to ascribe inerrancy to a map, then, and quite another to know how to interpret it. To understand a map, you need to know its conventions. For example, you need to know the scale. You also need to know the key that explains how to read the various symbols used by the cartographer to represent places like rivers and cities. Finally, you need to know the legend, which is a way of imagining the world. The Bible is composed of different kinds of literature, each of which maps the theodrama in a distinctive way. Yet all the maps are reliable: they correspond—in different ways!—to this or that aspect of what is really the case. They are not only compatible but complement one another. Maps are no good, however, unless you are oriented. The Rule of Faith serves as a kind of compass in this regard, reminding us that all the biblical maps ultimately point in the same "Christotelic" direction.[46] The canon is a unique compass that points not to the north but to the church's North Star: Jesus Christ, the alpha and omega of the whole theodrama.

V. TRUTH AND INTERPRETATION: THE PROCESS

The Bible is discourse (what is written) on a marvelous matter (what is written about). Faith seeking understanding means attending to the evangelical (canonical) discourse about the evangelical (Christological, ultimately) subject matter. Interpretation is the process of discerning the truth of the matter from the discourse. At what stage in the process of interpretation do we arrive at truth? Doing justice to this question means espousing a three-dimensional view of truth that does justice to the world behind, of, and in front of the text; and this means preserving the ties that bind history, literature, and Christian faith.

1. *Truth behind the text: historical excavation (history as truth-bearer).* In the first place, the theodrama involves the words and acts of God in history. But this does not mean that theological interpretation of Scripture should come to resemble an archaeological dig.

The text is not simply a means to an end. We err in treating the text merely as evidence with which to reconstruct "what actually happened." On the contrary, our focus as interpreters must be on the biblical witness. God's word is *in* history but not *of* it. What we know of the historical context (which includes what we know of the state of the Hebrew or Greek language at a given time and place) serves as corroborative evidence for determining what the author is saying. Historical reconstruction is helpful when it helps to clarify the authorial discourse (e.g., what the author was doing in tending to or using just these words in just this fashion). Historical reconstruction becomes problematic when re-creating "what actually happened" becomes more important than attending to the biblical witness. And it is distinctly unhelpful when the desire for historical accuracy causes us to miss what the biblical authors are actually doing with their texts.

Take, for example, the urge to harmonize apparent historical discrepancies. Modern harmonizations seek to fit the events recounted in the four Gospels into an exact chronological sequence. The very attempt begs the question as to whether the evangelists were primarily interested in chronology. Interestingly, Calvin wrote a Harmony of the Gospels too, but he admits that chronological precision was not the goal of the authors.[47] He is content to display the differences between the accounts. It is a true harmony where the voices do not sing in unison but take different parts in order to weave a richer, fuller texture.

History, strictly speaking, is a form of literature; it is someone's testimony to the past: "That which we have heard, which we have seen with our eyes . . . and have touched with our hands, concerning the word of life" (1 John 1:1). Biblical narrative is a species of theodramatic history: history told with the confessional purpose of highlighting the divine word and the divine deed. Unlike chronology, which simply lists events in succession, history narrates events, selecting and ordering and highlighting in order to make sense of the succession. It follows that "literary understanding is a necessary condition of historical understanding."[48] The historical truth claims of the Bible "will never be rightly understood unless the literary mode of their representation is itself understood."[49] The narrative form of history is not just packaging; it is a form of understanding, what

Ricoeur calls "explanation by emplotment." And what is true of history is true, I believe, for all subject matters on which the biblical authors discourse as well. In short: our access to the referent of the text is through the text.[50]

2. *Truth of the text: textual exposition (literature as truth-bearer).* The second, textual dimension of biblical truth is the crucial one, for both authorial discourse and subject matter are textually mediated. The truth of the text is not divorced from history; it is the royal, or should I say prophetic and apostolic, road to history: not to history behind the text, as if we could detach the meaning of the events from their confessional framework, but to history as seen (rightly and truly, I might add) through the text.

a. *Discourse on matter: how authors do things with biblical texts.* Though it is pious and understandable, it can be misleading to insist that every "word" of the Bible is true. Strictly speaking, words alone are neither true nor false; they don't mean anything until someone uses them in a stretch of discourse to say something. This claim has an enormous bearing on our subject because it directs our attention as interpreters not to isolated words but to larger literary units. To speak of truth in interpretation, then, is to put the focus squarely on discourse. Discourse is someone saying something about something to someone, and hermeneutics is the art of discerning the discourse in written works.

The Chicago Statement affirms the truth of Scripture "on all matters" that it addresses (Art. IX, XI). As we have seen, there is no one uniform way in which the biblical authors address their subject matter. We therefore need to add another phrase to our definition of discourse: what someone says in some way about something to someone. "In some way." We read in Hebrews that God has spoken in former times in diverse ways, but now he has spoken by his Son. I submit that in Scripture

God continues to speak to us in diverse ways—to be precise, in and through different forms of discourse and different literary forms. The present section will focus on discourse, the next on literary forms.

The Lausanne Covenant (1974) and the Chicago Statement (1978) use similar formulations to define biblical inerrancy, the one saying the Bible is "without error in all that it affirms," the other that "it is true and reliable in all matters it addresses" (Art. XI). Strictly speaking, however, it neither affirms nor addresses; authors do. Interestingly, Carl Henry worries that too great a focus on authorial intention detracts from inerrancy, since "some commentators seem to imply that the biblical writers need not always have intended to teach the truth."[51] For example, does the author of Joshua 9:13 intend his statement about the sun standing still to contradict a heliocentric worldview? Was Melanchthon right to attack Copernicus for suggesting that it is the earth, not the sun, that moves?[52]

Everything hinges on the notion of "affirming" and "addressing." Joshua mentions the sun standing still; but is this what the narrative affirms? Is not Joshua rather affirming, in a manner that his readers could understand, that God supernaturally intervened on behalf of Israel? The point is that he is employing phenomenal language (e.g., everyday language about the everyday world) in order to communicate. To press Joshua 9 into the service of Ptolemaic science would be an odd use indeed of the passage. Why? Because the point of the passage lies elsewhere. To be precise, it is a theological and, yes, historical (but not astronomical) point.

This example signals the importance of the distinction between locutions and illocutions. A locutionary act is the act of saying something by uttering or writing words; an illocutionary act is what one does by means of such locutionary acts. For example, the locutionary act sets forth propositional content (e.g., "sun"; "standing"; "still"); the illocutionary act does something with it (e.g., asks, states, promises, commands: "Is the sun standing still?"; "The sun stands still"; "Sun, stand still!" etc.). What the author is doing in Joshua 9 is narrating history in order to display how God has made good on his promise to Israel to bestow the Promised Land. As in other instances of God making himself known, here too we would do well to employ Calvin's notion of "accommodation": the story of the sun standing still is an example of God using baby talk, adapting his communication in order that it be intelligible to finite, historically-conditioned creatures.[53] God stoops to speak and show.

The biblical authors did not intend every one of their sentences to be an assertive statement. To return to Joshua 9: the author's use of phenomenal language is merely background scenery for what really matters, the theodramatic assertion about the act of God in history. Some draw from examples such as Joshua 9 the inference that God accommodates fallen (and thus errant) human interpretative horizons and then conclude that Scripture "contains" error even if it does not "teach" it.[54] But we need not go so far if we distinguish locutions from illocutions, what one says from what one is doing by means of one's words.

Such a distinction would also have helped Carl Henry to integrate authorial intention into his understanding of inerrancy. As indicated above, Henry was leery of suggesting that the biblical authors did not always intend to teach truth: "Does not the appeal simply to authorial intention leave us with no criterion for distinguishing within any biblical writer's communication when and where he inerrantly teaches factual truth or merely inerrantly transmits an errant content?"[55] Yet as we have seen, the task of the interpreter is precisely to discern the authorial discourse in the written work, as Henry himself later tacitly acknowledges when he explains that inerrancy implies that truth attaches itself not only to the theological teaching of the Bible "but also to historical and scientific matters insofar as they are part of the express message of the inspired writings."[56] "Express message" is a somewhat circuitous way of talking about authorial assertives.[57] In treating "truth and interpretation," then, it is crucial to acknowledge that authors can do more than one thing with their texts. In particular, we must be careful not to confuse using phenomenal language (locutions) with affirming the phenomena (a specific illocution).

b. *The cognitive contribution of literary forms: the literal sense is the literary sense.* The Bible proposes things for our consideration not just via individual assertions but "in many ways" that derive from its diverse literary forms (as well as from its diverse illocutionary forces, as we have just seen). The form of what Scripture says is not merely incidental to its truth. I am thus a modified propositionalist. I recognize the cognitive significance not only of statements and propositions but of all the Bible's figures of speech and literary forms. Yet I resist the temptation to dedramatize—to de-form!—the biblical text in order to abstract a revealed truth. My approach to theology—call it "postconservative"—does not deny the importance of cognitive content, but it does resist privileging a single form—the propositional statement—for expressing it.[58]

It is Scripture that reveals God, not a set of detached propositions. Revealed truths are not abstract but canonically concrete. This is our evangelical birthright—truth in all its canonical radiance, not a diluted mess of propositionalist pottage. In my more optimistic moments, I wonder whether the recovery of the Bible's literary forms might galvanize a new reformation as did the recovery of the original languages of the Bible.

The Bible speaks truly in all that it literally affirms. It is an egregious mistake, however, to identify the literal with the literalistic sense of Scripture, that is, with the empirical object or state of affairs to which it refers. The literal sense of Scripture as a whole is the theodramatic sense—God's words and acts, especially as these coalesce in Christ—but the way the Bible is about these acts is not always narrowly historical, literalistic, or analytic.

That the literal sense is the literary sense has important consequences for inerrancy. What, after all, is an error? Simply to speak of a factual mistake does not get us very far. What are mistakes, and how do we recognize them? What in one context might count as an error is another person's best estimate. Errors, then, are relative to the kind of claim being made. We can only assess success and failure if we know what kind of claim is being made.[59] This is precisely where literary forms become important. Our expectations as to what kind of claim is being made in a text must line up with what kind of claim the text is making. If a text makes no claim to chronological accuracy, then chronological inaccuracy is no error. Different kinds of texts aim at different kinds of precision. Poetry is precise—it demands just the right word in just the right order—but its precision is of a different nature than the precision we expect in modern history or science. If biblical narrative is primarily interested in recounting key scenes in the theodrama, we should exercise caution before rushing to the assumption that the biblical authors worked with the same standards of historiography as reporters at the *New York Times* (bad example!).

In championing literary form, I am not saying, "choose this day whom you shall serve, history or fiction." Don't confuse my position with that of Marcus Borg who defines taking the Bible seriously but not literally in terms of the ability to hear the biblical stories once again as true stories, even as one knows that they may not be factually true and that their truth does not depend on their factuality.[60] By contrast, I believe that taking the

Bible seriously requires us to take the Bible literally, that is, in its literary sense.

   c. *Doctrine and the role of the canonically-formed theodramatic imagination.* Even philosophers who previously had nothing but disdain for figures of speech have recently come to appreciate the cognitive significance of metaphors, narratives, and other literary forms. Martha Nussbaum, for instance, says that "[l]iterary form is not separable from philosophical content, but is, itself, a part of content—an integral part, then, of the search for and the statement of truth."[61] Narratives do more than convey propositions; they configure the past in a certain way and say, "look at the world like this." They do not merely inform; they train us to see the world in certain ways, theodramatic ways. And this brings me to the role of the imagination in interpreting biblical truth.

   For too long evangelical scholarship has given the imagination a bad rap. To be sure, there are vain imaginings. But this no more disqualifies the imagination per se from theological service than logical fallacies disqualify reason. A false picture of the imagination as the power of conjuring up things that are not really there has for too long held us captive.

   By imagination I mean the power of synoptic vision—the ability to synthesize heterogeneous elements into a unity. The imagination is a cognitive faculty by which we see as whole what those without imagination see only as unrelated parts. Stories display the imagination in action, for it is the role of the plot (*mythos*) to unify various persons and events in a single story with a beginning, middle, and end. Where reason analyzes, breaking things (and texts) up into their constituent parts, imagination synthesizes, making connections between things that appear unrelated.

   The purpose of exegesis is not to excavate but to explore canonically-embodied truth by becoming apprentices to the lit-

erary forms, and this involves more than mastering the propositional content. By learning imaginatively to follow and indwell
the biblical texts, we see through them to reality as it really is
"in Christ."

As C. S. Lewis knew, stories too are truth-bearers that
enable us both to "taste" and to "see," or better, to experience
as concrete what can otherwise be understood only as an
abstraction. What gets conveyed through stories, then, is not
simply the proposition but something of the reality itself. For
example, the biblical narrative does not simply convey information about God but displays God's triune identity itself as it
is manifest through the creative and redemptive work of his two
hands. One can state that "God is good" in a proposition, but
it takes a narrative to "taste and see that the Lord is good."
Similarly, to see the church as the body of Christ is a rich cognitive insight, but it cannot be paraphrased propositionally
without something vital getting lost in interpretation.

The theological interpreter inhabits the world of the biblical text—not some cleverly devised modern or postmodern
myths, but true myth, myth become redemptive history, myth
become—dare I say it?—fact. But we only get to the fact through
the forms of its literary incarnation. And what literary genres
communicate is not simply propositional content but ways of
processing this content into meaningful wholes: ways of thinking, seeing, and even experiencing this content. Theological
interpretation involves nothing less than the ability to
see/feel/taste the truth borne by Scripture's literary forms.

The truth of God's word is not merely propositional, then,
but richly propositional. Scripture summons the intellect to
accept its rendering of reality, but it also summons the imagination to see, feel, and taste the goodness of God. We need the
diversity of biblical genres fully to understand the theodrama
and our part in it. When we learn to see, feel, think, and indwell

the biblical texts, interpretation becomes a matter not only of information but of personal formation: of learning how to speak and act in a way that accords with the real "in Christ."

3. *Truth "in front of" the text: engaging the matter (the reader as truth-bearer).* To speak of the truth in front of the text is to focus on the reader's engagement with its subject matter. It is here that emergent evangelicals have something to contribute, not by way of a replacement but by way of a corrective to the conservative evangelical emphasis on propositional truth.

a. *Truth is (inter)subjectivity: covenantal correspondence.* Kierkegaard famously commented that truth is subjectivity. He was not espousing relativism, only calling for individuals to commit themselves passionately to the truth. Objective truth denotes "what is" regardless of one's relation to it; what Kierkegaard calls subjective truth, by contrast, denotes how "what is" has an existential bearing on the life of the one who commits to it. Kierkegaard well knew that the NT is easy enough to understand (in theory), but difficult to understand in practice, for the latter requires obedience.

Stated differently: the correspondence that ultimately counts in biblical interpretation is not simply that of sentences but of oneself. The truth of the Bible lays claim not only to our heads but to our hearts and our hands. To come to Scripture is to be confronted with a truth that is both objective and rational on the one hand and personal and relational on the other. Emergent evangelicals are right to remind us that "[t]he idea of God as an entity knowable by propositional analysis is metaphysical, a survival of heathen philosophy."[62] But they are wrong to suggest that a personal, relational, and covenantal knowing of God excludes a propositional component. Indeed, to say, "We must treat Scripture not as facticity but as address"[63] is to invoke just the kind of stultifying binary hierarchical opposition from which postmodernity was supposed to have liberated us! Surely the

way to break down the dividing wall of methodological hostility between conservative and emergent evangelical is to recognize that each side has a valid point. God's word is both personal
and propositional: the Bible is a book of speech acts through
which the divine authorial agent personally relates to readers
precisely by doing things with propositions (e.g., commanding,
asserting, promising).

God is the paradigmatic communicative agent, and his word
is true because it is absolutely reliable. There is a correspondence
between what he says, what he does, and who he is. Jesus Christ
is the truth because he is God-keeping-his-word; as God's
"kept" word, Christ not only bears but is the truth, a personal
bearer of the way God is. Truth in the context of theological
interpretation must never be merely theoretical (a mere correspondence relation) but practical, transformative, and relational
(a covenantal relation). We enter into the covenantal relation of
truth when our words, thoughts, and deeds conform to the
image of the one who is the truth incarnate.

b. *Creative understanding: interpretative traditions as bearers of truth?* It is the interpreter Spirit who illumines readers to
discern the true subject matter of Scripture and who enables
covenantal correspondence, establishing cognitive and relational contact between the reader, what is written, and what is
written about. The Spirit guides the church into all truth. Just
as redemption has a history, so perhaps we can speak of the
progress of illumination, and identify it with church tradition.
Tradition is a means of nurture, but it cannot be our final norm;
Scripture itself performs this role. We do well to recall
Augustine's warning: "If we are to look back to long custom or
antiquity alone, then also murderers and adulterers, and similar
persons can defend their crimes in this way, because they are
ancient."[64] Calvin, likewise, reminds us that truth cannot be

determined by long-standing custom only, for this is just "the conspiracy of men."[65]

Truth is one, yet there are multiple interpretative traditions. Is there one true interpretation for all time, one true way only of witnessing to biblical truth? If doctrine gives direction for our fitting participation in the theodrama, then we need to have local as well as biblical knowledge in order to know what to say and how to act in particular situations when confronted with problems not explicitly addressed in Scripture. Andrew Lincoln expresses the tension well in his splendid book *Truth on Trial*, a study of the trial narrative in the Fourth Gospel: "These two interrelated aspects of witnessing—the requirement of attesting to a reality that is beyond oneself but also the ability to do this only in terms of one's own contextually conditioned perspective—are a reminder of the dialectical nature of theological interpretation."[66] The task, in short, is to give faithful and creative witness to biblical truth, to make judgments that fit with our script and with our situation. It takes many interpreters and interpretative traditions fully to appreciate and understand the divine discourse, just as it takes four Gospels fully to render the reality of Jesus Christ.

c. *Truth as eschatological correspondence to the already and not yet.* I am attempting to broaden our sense of truth as correspondence for the sake of enriching the ministry of doctrine and of reorienting our theology toward wisdom rather than mere information and knowledge. The wise person is the one who understands and participates fittingly in the created and redeemed order. We get wisdom by letting the biblical texts train our imaginations to see how things fit together theodramatically. The purpose of sound doctrine is to enable pilgrims to make covenantal contact and to live in theodramatic correspondence with reality.

It only remains to add that theodramatic truth is ultimately a matter of eschatological correspondence. Doctrinal truth is what corresponds to or "fits" the already/not-yet contours of the theodrama. On the one hand, doctrine displays an "already-correspondence" to what God has done in Christ. On the other hand, doctrine is about what God is now doing in the Spirit, namely, making all things new in Christ. Doctrine captures this not-yet aspect of truth by directing us to become what we already are.

Theodramatic correspondence is an eschatological affair, in the sense that most of the key scenes of the theodrama have already been played, though some (including the ones we play next) are not yet concluded. Doctrine directs disciples to speak and act in such a way that those scenes that have "not yet" been performed correspond to those that have been performed "already."

To interpret the Bible in Spirit and in truth means following doctrine's direction, in both senses of the term: theatric and cartographic. The point is to practice as well as preach doctrinal truth, to walk the way of Jesus Christ, to continue the theodrama into new scenes, and so embody Christian wisdom.

VI. Conclusion: Truth and Interpretation— The Next Step

1. *At home with the interpreter.* So, what did Christian actually see in the House of the Interpreter? He saw the virtue of Patience extolled. Truth is the daughter of time, it has been said, and this is a good argument for attending to catholicity, the tradition of interpretation passed on through the centuries. Sometimes the desire for certainty can be a form of impatience for the truth.

Christian also saw what should be a sobering sight for us: a professor—thankfully Bunyan does not give his area of specialization!—in an iron cage, a man in despair who has missed the way; one who is lost in misinterpretation.

He saw a vision of the Last Judgment, where he discovers that the only wholly reliable reader of the text is the one who is its author. This picture extols the virtue of hermeneutical humility.[67]

Finally, Christian saw the picture of a man with his eyes lifted up to heaven, the best of books in his hand, the law of truth written upon his lips. The Interpreter tells Christian that this is "the only man whom the Lord of the place whither thou art going hath authorized to be thy Guide." He sees Christ, the way, the life, the ultimate interpreter of truth.

2. *Walking the way of biblical truth: a new itinerary for inerrancy?* The Bible's authority covers more than the propositional content it conveys, important though that aspect is. Thanks to the diversity of its forms, the Bible trains us to see and taste the world in terms of the canonical imagination and to make judgments that correspond to the already/not-yet nature of the theodrama. True doctrine corresponds to the theodrama and directs us to do the same. We best put ourselves in the way of truth when we interpret the Scriptures in their canonical context with the aid of the catholic tradition.

What is the moral of all this for inerrancy? I do not usually trade in etymologies, but I cannot help pointing out that "errancy"—as in "knight errant"—is related to the Latin *errare* ("to stray"), which in turn is related to the term "itinerary." Inerrancy is first cousin to itinerary, and this reminds us that Scripture reliably maps the way of Jesus Christ, not as a theological Euclid—a book of abstract propositions—but as a book of theodramatic wisdom. The Bible is wholly trustworthy and true because its direction is wholly reliable.

Perhaps we need to rehabilitate the classic term "infallibility" to make sure that theological interpreters of Scripture do not become mere information processors. Inerrancy is most appropriate as a description of biblical assertions. Yet we need to recognize that everything God does with the propositional content of Scripture—warning, promising, commanding, and yes, asserting—is of theological significance. When properly interpreted, the Scriptures are utterly reliable because they are infallible—not liable to fail—no matter what God is doing in them. Recall the words of the prophet Isaiah in 55:11: "My word . . . shall not return to me empty, but it shall accomplish that which I purpose." What is this purpose? The ultimate purpose of Scripture is to draw us into the drama of redemption, into the life and action of the triune God, so that we can be faithful yet creative actors who glorify God in all that we say and do. I trust that emergent and conservative evangelicals can agree on that!

Whatever term we employ to affirm the supreme authority of Scripture, we had better exercise caution before buying into philosophical theories that dilute the richness of its truth. Raschke exhorts us to "dehellenize" evangelical faith. To the extent that evangelical formulations of inerrancy have fallen prey to a modern philosophical captivity of the word, his warning is well-taken. On the other hand, there is nothing to be gained simply by exchanging masters! Evangelicals should no more emerge out of postmodernity than out of modernity. On the contrary, we should be prepared to diverge from modernity and postmodernity alike in order to preserve the integrity of our witness to the truth of the gospel, and if this means "de-continentalizing" the faith, then so be it.[68]

It is time to regroup; evangelicals should diverge from modernity and postmodernity alike when these do not serve the gospel and instead converge in the great Protestant tradition where Scripture is the supreme rule for life and thought. And not only the Protestant tradition. Thomas Aquinas was willing to correct the philosophy of his day to make it biblical, too. Moreover, he viewed faith as both propositional and personal: "faith is believing God himself since the truths of faith are revealed by God."[69] Faith has a statable content, but the point of processing this information is to share in what God knows, to share in God's life, and to participate in the evangelical action.

3. *Pilgrims' practice: performing doctrinal truth truthfully.* The Christian pilgrim-interpreter is ultimately on a missionary journey. Just as Jesus' mission was to be God's truth claim to the world, so the mission of biblical interpreters is to bear witness to the truth of Jesus Christ in all that they say and do. The Christian truth claim is not a matter of the will to power but of the will to weakness, a matter of enduring all sorts of critical testing, epistemic and existential, just as Jesus endured the cross. Christian interpreters must speak the truth in love, do the truth in love, and suffer the truth in love.

I conclude my hermeneutic homily with a closing charge. True interpretation of the word of truth is an act of understanding that must be proved and exhibited in practice. It takes a company of pilgrims. Our life together in the church is our most eloquent commentary on the gospel and, as such, ought itself to be exhibit number one of Christian truth. At least, Paul thought so: "For it seems to me that God has put us apostles on display" (1 Cor. 4:9). As Christians and evangelicals, we are to be an exhibit—a spectacle (*theatron*) of truth to the watching world. May we all leave the House of the Interpreter refreshed, a great company of pilgrims, eager to take up our book and walk the way of truth and life.[70]

EPILOGUE

Andreas J. Köstenberger

Whatever happened to truth?" Look at him there, standing in front of Pilate, bearing witness to the truth, calmly stating that his kingdom is not of this world. "Behold, the man!" Here is the Truth, beaten and bruised for our sins, hung on a tree—look at him now, crucified.

Who would have thought? Truth is a person. What is more, truth is a *crucified* person, Jesus the Messiah, the one-of-a-kind, sent Son from the Father. Three days later, that Truth rose from the grave. Death could not keep him. He showed himself to many and is now exalted with God.

"Whatever happened to truth?" In one sense, the answer is, "The truth is just fine, thank you." Jesus, the Word, continues to speak to those with ears to hear in his word, the Scriptures. He has returned to his glory with the Father and awaits his return from there at the Father's appointed time.

In another sense, however, *truth is languishing in a state of crisis* in our day. In much of contemporary culture, truth has been supplanted by a kind of paranoia that is so skeptical toward any finality of knowing that it is prone to believe conspiracy theories, no matter how far-fetched (witness the *Da Vinci Code* phenomenon).[1] All of this contributes to a sense of uncertainty that holds that all knowledge is provisional and subject to constant revision as new facts surface that need to be considered. In this context, can truth, "true truth," to quote Francis

Schaeffer once again, long survive? Or is it time to declare the *death of truth* just as some declared (prematurely, one might add) the death of God in a previous generation?

If Jesus is the Truth, and in him the world's "truth" is crucified, the only way to recover truth in our day is by way of turning to the crucified Truth, the only "true truth" there is. "Jews demand signs and Greeks seek wisdom, but we preach Christ crucified": "Christ the power of God and the wisdom of God" (1 Cor. 1:22-23). As Adolf Schlatter wrote in one of the darkest hours for truth in living memory in 1937, "Do we know Jesus? If we no longer know him, we no longer know ourselves."[2]

In light of this, what did we learn from the essays in the present volume? First, we came to realize that truth is ultimately theocentric and Christocentric, even crucicentric. Truth is not found in human philosophy or religious imagination, but only in the words and acts of God, particularly as these are identified with the Bible and with Jesus Christ. It is this truth that Jesus declared before Pilate. As Pilate learned (or failed to learn) two millennia ago, and as thinkers as diverse as Rudolf Bultmann and C. S. Lewis reiterated in the more recent past, this truth, in turn, requires a decision. As Jesus asked his followers, "Who do *you* think that I am?" What will your and my answer be?

For those of us who have committed our lives to Christ, of course, this is only the beginning. We are now called to bear witness to the truth as Jesus did, and as a steady throng of his followers did throughout church history. Albert Mohler's essay furnishes a splendid example of what it means to engage in cultural analysis from a Christian point of view and to take the pulse of a world in which truth is in serious crisis. Mohler's spiritual diagnosis of our society is characterized by unusual clarity of vision and provides an excellent vantage point from which to engage our truth-deprived culture. According to Mohler, our world is plagued by the following six "Ds": a deconstruction of truth, the death of the meta-narrative, the demise of the text, the dominion of therapy, a decline in authority, and a displacement of morality. Dr. Mohler's own speaking ministry, his radio program, and his daily commentary (www.albertmohler.com) are a powerful demonstration of "Christianity confronting culture" by speaking the truth in love and yet doing so with deep conviction.

What else have we learned from reading this book? We have seen that postmodernism is not only intellectually bankrupt—and the Christian philosopher J. P. Moreland has cited at least five reasons why this is the case—but is also, in Moreland's terms, "a form of intellectual pacifism" that is "an immoral and cowardly viewpoint" that Christians must confront with love and clarity.

But how are some of the above insights to be translated into a proper approach to interpreting Scripture? We may know the truth, but how are we to derive it and demonstrate it responsibly from Scripture? Here the "Vanhoozer proposal" set forth in the final essay of the present volume truly breaks new ground. Vanhoozer starts out by showing the inadequacy of an exclusively propositionalist approach to Scripture, contending that the affirmation of inerrancy by itself does not yet represent a full-fledged hermeneutic. He goes on to argue for an approach that discerns biblical truth as expressed in the interface between an author's discourse, interpreted in context, and the way things are. In Vanhoozer's "synoptic vision," the Bible's meta-narrative is best described as a theodrama, presenting the creative and redemptive work of the triune God. The Bible, as it were, is the script providing us with performance knowledge as participants in that theodrama in our day.

Vanhoozer also advances our understanding of the often-debated interface between history and literature. "What we know of the historical context," he writes, "serves as *corroborative evidence* for determining what the author is saying" (my emphasis). "Historical reconstruction is helpful when it helps clarify the authorial discourse." Hence, over against those who hold to a form of textual autonomy (the notion that "the text is all there is" as far as interpretation is concerned), Vanhoozer asserts that, within the framework of a hermeneutic aimed at discerning the authorial intent as expressed in a given text or discourse, historical work, both linguistic and otherwise, can be a useful interpretive tool. Despite the abuses of the "historical-critical method" in the hands of anti-supernaturalist, skeptical-critical practitioners, history and literature should not be pitted against each other.

In fact, Vanhoozer, in a bold section of his work, proposes that history-writing should be viewed as "a form of literature" in that it represents someone's testimony to the past (citing 1 John 1:1). History narrates events; thus "*literary understanding is a necessary condition of historical understanding.*" The narrative form of history is therefore in itself a form of understanding. For this reason, to supply Vanhoozer with yet another biblical allusion to bolster his argument (not that he needs one), "What God has joined together [i.e., history and literature], let man not put asunder"—and that includes the practitioners of historical criticism and literary critics alike.

There is one more important contribution. In underscoring the importance of interpreting Scripture genre-sensitively—over against the proponents of a "propositionalist" approach who tend to flatten the genre diversity of Scripture—Vanhoozer uses the analogy of interpreting Scripture and reading a variety of maps. The important question, Vanhoozer contends, is to discern what kind of map we are dealing with in a given instance. Maps normally do not describe reality in a "picture-perfect" type of way (e.g., the map of the Paris métro uses color-coding for the different lines, but the actual rails are not color-coded). The question therefore is, "What *type of representation* does a given map—or in the case of Scripture, a given genre of Scripture—use?" (my emphasis). Vanhoozer expresses the hope that learning this lesson may spark a revolution in the area of biblical interpretation similar to the one galvanized by the recovery of the original languages of the Bible.

We started our discussion by citing the words of Francis Schaeffer, calling evangelicals to "take a stand for biblical truth and morality in the full spectrum of life." The present volume represents a modest effort to do just that, addressing the question of truth in our day from a biblical, cultural, philosophical, and hermeneutical perspective. The contributions to this volume have been both deconstructive and reconstructive. We have sought to deconstruct postmodernism (turning the tables—ha!) and have attempted to point forward to a better way of discerning truth in Scripture, one that is *respectful* of the rights of the biblical authors and *responsible* in its dealing with the scriptural texts in the diversity of their literary genres.

We realize that this hardly represents the final word in the contemporary hermeneutical debate and are looking forward to further discussion on the four major angles of the issue of truth discussed in the present volume: Jesus as the representative and embodiment of truth; the importance of cultural analysis, critique, and engagement; the deconstruction of postmodernism; and the "Vanhoozer proposal" of a theodramatic hermeneutic.[3]

Yet while the final word has not yet been spoken in the contemporary hermeneutical debate, we believe that the final word has indeed been spoken in the history of God's dealings with humanity. With the biblical authors, we believe that in Jesus, all of God's promises are "yes" and "amen." And while now we see in a mirror dimly, one day we will see Truth face to face. That Truth, indeed, is a person, and his name is Jesus Christ. And in keeping with biblical testimony, at the sight of Jesus every knee will bow and every tongue confess that Jesus Christ is Lord to the glory of God the Father. May it be so, now and forever. Amen.

FOR FURTHER READING

Blackburn, Simon and Keith Simmons, eds. *Truth*. Oxford Readings in Philosophy. Oxford/New York: Oxford University Press, 1999.

Bock, Darrell L. *Purpose-Directed Theology: Getting Our Priorities Right in Evangelical Controversies*. Downers Grove, IL: InterVarsity, 2002.

Brown, Harold O. J. *The Sensate Culture: Western Civilization Between Chaos and Transformation*. Dallas: Word, 1996.

Carson, D. A., ed. *Telling the Truth: Evangelizing Postmoderns*. Grand Rapids: Zondervan, 2000.

_____. *The Gagging of God: Christianity Confronts Pluralism*. Grand Rapids: Zondervan, 1996.

_____ and John D. Woodbridge, eds. *God and Culture: Essays in Honor of Carl F. H. Henry*. Grand Rapids: Eerdmans, 1993.

Colson, Charles with Ellen Santilli Vaughn. *Against the Night: Living in the New Dark Ages*. Ann Arbor, MI: Servant, 1989.

_____ with Nancy Pearcey. *How Now Shall We Live?* Wheaton: Tyndale House, 1999.

Craig, William Lane. *Reasonable Truth: Christian Truth and Apologetics*. Wheaton: Crossway, 1994.

Dockery, David S., ed. *The Challenge of Postmodernism: An Evangelical Engagement*. Wheaton: Victor, 1995.

Erickson, Millard J. *Postmodernizing the Faith: Evangelical Responses to the Challenge of Postmodernism*. Grand Rapids: Baker, 1998.

_____. *Truth or Consequences: The Promise and Perils of Postmodernism*. Downers Grove, IL: InterVarsity, 2001.

_____, Paul Kjöss Helseth, and Justin Taylor, eds. *Reclaiming the Center: Confronting Evangelical Accommodation in Postmodern Times.* Wheaton: Crossway, 2004.

Greer, Robert C. *Mapping Postmodernism: A Survey of Christian Options.* Downers Grove, IL: InterVarsity, 2003.

Grenz, Stanley J. *A Primer on Postmodernism.* Grand Rapids: Eerdmans, 1996.

Groothuis, Douglas R. *Truth Decay: Defending Christianity Against the Challenges of Postmodernism.* Downers Grove, IL: InterVarsity, 2000.

Heimbach, Daniel R. *True Sexual Morality: Recovering Biblical Standards for a Culture in Crisis.* Wheaton: Crossway, 2004.

Henry, Carl F. H. *Twilight of a Great Civilization: The Drift Toward Paganism.* Wheaton: Crossway, 1988.

_____. *Toward a Recovery of Christian Belief.* Wheaton: Crossway, 1990.

Hicks, Peter. *Evangelicals and Truth: A Creative Proposal for a Postmodern Age.* Leicester: Apollos, 1998.

Köstenberger, Andreas J. with David J. Jones. *God, Marriage & Family: Rebuilding the Biblical Foundation.* Wheaton: Crossway, 2004.

Liefeld, David R. "God's Word or Male Words? Postmodern Conspiracy Culture and Feminist Myths of Christian Origins." *Journal of the Evangelical Theological Society* 48, No. 3 (2005): 449-473.

Lincoln, Andrew T. *Truth on Trial: The Lawsuit Motif in the Fourth Gospel.* Peabody, MA: Hendrickson, 2000.

Lindsley, Arthur William. *True Truth: Defending Absolute Truth in a Relativistic Age.* Downers Grove, IL: InterVarsity, 2004.

Lyotard, Jean-François. *The Postmodern Condition: A Report on Knowledge.* Translated by Geoff Bennington and Brian Massumi. Minneapolis: University of Minnesota Press, 1984.

McGrath, Alister E. *A Passion for Truth: The Intellectual Coherence of Evangelicalism.* Downers Grove, IL: InterVarsity, 1996.

Meek, Esther. *Longing to Know: The Philosophy of Knowledge for Ordinary People*. Grand Rapids: Brazos, 2003.

Moreland, J. P. and William Lane Craig. *Philosophical Foundations for a Christian Worldview*. Downers Grove, IL: InterVarsity, 2003.

Netland, Harold A. *Dissonant Voices: Religious Pluralism and the Question of Truth*. Grand Rapids: Eerdmans, 1991.

Nicole, Roger. "The Biblical Concept of Truth," 287-298, in *Scripture and Truth*. Edited by D. A. Carson and John D. Woodbridge. Grand Rapids: Baker, 1992.

Osborne, Grant R. *The Hermeneutical Spiral: A Comprehensive Introduction to Biblical Interpretation*. Downers Grove, IL: InterVarsity, 1991.

Pearcey, Nancy R. *Total Truth: Liberating Christianity from Its Cultural Captivity*. Wheaton: Crossway, 2004.

Schaeffer, Francis A. *The Complete Works of Francis Schaeffer*. 5 vols. Wheaton: Crossway, 1982.

Thiselton, Anthony C. "Truth," 874-902, in *New International Dictionary of New Testament Theology*. Vol. 3. Edited by Colin Brown. Grand Rapids: Zondervan, 1986.

Vanhoozer, Kevin J. *Is There a Meaning in This Text? The Bible, The Reader, and the Morality of Literary Knowledge*. Grand Rapids: Zondervan, 1998.

_____. *First Theology: God, Scripture & Hermeneutics*. Downers Grove, IL: InterVarsity, 2002.

_____. *The Drama of Doctrine: A Canonical-Linguistic Approach to Christian Theology*. Louisville: Westminster John Knox, 2005.

Volf, Miroslav. *Exclusion & Embrace: A Theological Exploration of Identity, Otherness, and Reconciliation*. Nashville: Abingdon, 1996.

Wells, David F. *No Place for Truth or Whatever Happened to Evangelical Theology?* Grand Rapids: Eerdmans, 1993.

_____. *God in the Wasteland: The Reality of Truth in a World of Fading Dreams*. Grand Rapids: Eerdmans, 1994.

NOTES

INTRODUCTION

1. Cf. Francis Schaeffer, *Whatever Happened to the Human Race?* in *The Complete Works of Francis Schaeffer*, Vol. 5 (Wheaton: Crossway, 1982), co-written with C. Everett Koop, in which Schaeffer deals with scourges such as abortion and euthanasia.

2. E.g., Francis Schaeffer, *Escape from Reason*, in *Complete Works*, Vol. 1, 218-219, where Schaeffer writes, "It is an important principle to remember . . . that . . . though we do not have exhaustive truth, we have from the Bible what I term 'true truth.' In this way we know true truth about God, true truth about man and something truly about nature. Thus on the basis of the Scriptures, while we do not have exhaustive knowledge, we have true and unified knowledge."

3. Ibid., 233. For an assessment of Schaeffer's work, see the theme issue, "The Legacy of Francis Schaeffer," *Southern Baptist Journal of Theology* 6 (Summer 2002).

4. Francis Schaeffer, *Death in the City*, in *Complete Works*, Vol. 4, 230.

5. Francis Schaeffer, *The Great Evangelical Disaster*, in *Complete Works*, Vol. 4, 401.

6. See also the comparable challenges issued by Carl F. H. Henry in many of his works, including *Twilight of a Great Civilization: The Drift Toward Paganism* (Wheaton: Crossway, 1988) and *Toward a Recovery of Christian Belief* (Wheaton: Crossway, 1990); and by Charles Colson, with Nancy Pearcey, *How Now Shall We Live?* (Wheaton: Tyndale House, 1999, alluding to Schaeffer's *How Shall We Then Live?*) and with Ellen Santilli Vaughn, *Against the Night: Living in the New Dark Ages* (Ann Arbor, MI: Servant, 1989). But note the critique of Schaeffer, Henry, and Colson as engaging in "cultural pessimism" by James A. Patterson, "Cultural Pessimism in Modern Evangelical Thought: Francis Schaeffer, Carl Henry, and Charles Colson," *JETS* (forthcoming).

7. For good examples, see David F. Wells, *No Place for Truth or Whatever Happened to Evangelical Theology?* (Grand Rapids: Eerdmans, 1993) and *God in the Wasteland: The Reality of Truth in a World of Fading Dreams* (Grand Rapids: Eerdmans, 1994); and Douglas Groothuis, *Truth Decay:*

Defending Christianity against the Challenges of Postmodernism (Downers Grove, IL: InterVarsity, 2000).

8. Emphasis added.

CHAPTER ONE: "WHAT IS TRUTH?" PILATE'S QUESTION IN ITS JOHANNINE AND LARGER BIBLICAL CONTEXT

1. Or, perhaps, with George R. Beasley-Murray, *John* (WBC 36; rev. ed.; Waco, TX: Word, 1999), 332: "Truth—what is that?!" As Ernst Haenchen, *A Commentary on the Gospel of John* (trans. Robert W. Funk; ed. Robert W. Funk with Ulrich Busse; Hermeneia Commentary Series [Philadelphia: Fortress, 1984], 2:180 (cited in ibid.) observes, "If Pilate now asks, when face to face with this truth, the truth that stands before him, 'What is truth?,' it is clear that Pilate does not belong among those whom 'the Father has given to Jesus.'" There is a good possibility that Pilate and Jesus discoursed in Greek, the *lingua franca* of the day, which would have provided common ground between Pilate, who spoke Latin, and Jesus, who spoke Aramaic. Cf. Craig L. Keener, *The Gospel of John: A Commentary* (Peabody, MA: Hendricksen, 2003), 2:1113: "Presumably Jesus and Pilate converse in Greek, the *lingua franca* of the Eastern empire, known to all educated Romans."

2. The Scripture quotations in this chapter are from the English Standard Version unless otherwise indicated.

3. Darrell L. Bock, *Jesus According to Scripture: Restoring the Portrait from the Gospels* (Grand Rapids— Baker, 2002), 525, reflects the scholarly consensus, dividing John 18—19 as follows: (1) Jesus' arrest and appearance before Annas, with Peter's denials (18:1-27); (2) Jesus' trial before Pilate (18:28—19:16a); and (3) Jesus' crucifixion, death, and burial (19:16b-42).

4. E.g., Gen. 24:27, 48; 32:10; 47:29; Exod. 28:26; Deut. 22:20; 33:8; Josh. 2:14; Judg. 9:15; etc. Keener, *John*, 1:418, notes that 90 percent of the instances of *alētheia* in the LXX translate the Hebrew *'emeth* and concludes that "'truth' often includes the sense of 'covenant faithfulness' in the Fourth Gospel."

5. E.g., Marcus Aurelius 9.1.2. See the discussion in Keener, *John*, 1:417-419.

6. E.g., Cicero, Inv. 2.53.161. A possible parallel to the present passage is Cicero, *Nat. Deor.* 1.67: *sed ubi est veritas?* ("But where is truth?"). Cited in *Neuer Wettstein: Texte zum Neuen Testament aus Griechentum und Hellenismus*, Band I/2: *Texte zum Johannesevangelium* (ed. Udo Schnelle; Berlin/New York: Walter de Gruyter, 2001), 795.

7. On "truth" in the OT, see the paper on this topic presented by Ronald Youngblood at the 2004 ETS annual meeting in San Antonio, Texas. There is some debate as to whether *'emeth* and *'emunah* are both to be construed as conveying the notion of faithfulness. Some equate the meaning of these expressions (e.g., R. W. L. Moberly, "אמן," *NIDOTTE*, 1:427-433; Willem

A. VanGemeren, *Psalms* [EBC 5; Grand Rapids: Zondervan, 1991], 235-236); others steadfastly insist on differentiating between the meaning of the two words (e.g., Alfred Jepsen, *TDOT*, 1:309-320; Hermann Cremer, *Biblico-Theological Lexicon of New Testament Greek* [4th ed.; trans. William Urwick; Edinburgh: T. & T. Clark, 1895], 627-630). In any case, God is both a God of truth (Exod. 31:6) and faithfulness (Lam. 3:22-23), and similar conduct is expected of the believer (Ps. 40:10-11).

8. When Jesus spoke to Pilate about a "kingdom" of truth, Pilate most likely would have thought of a kingdom of philosophers (e.g., Epictetus, *Diatr.* 3.22.49; Plutarch, *Flatterer* 16; Mor. 58E), who hardly ever challenged the security of the state. Keener, *John*, 1:418, says the "aborted dialogue of John 18:37-38 even suggests that John is aware of competing cultural epistemologies or understandings of truth."

9. The breakdown is as follows: *alētheia*: John 25, Synoptics 7; *alēthes*: John 14, Synoptics 2; *alēthinos*: John 9, Synoptics 1.

10. For a helpful study of truth in John's Gospel, see Scott Rupert Swain, "Truth in the Gospel of John" (Th.M. thesis; Southeastern Baptist Theological Seminary, 1998). See also the fine study by Dennis R. Lindsay, "What Is Truth? Ἀλήθεια in the Gospel of John," *ResQ* 35 (1993), 129-145; as well as S. Aalen, "'Truth,' a Key Word in St. John's Gospel," *SE* 2 (ed. Frank L. Cross; Berlin: Akademie, 1964), 3-24; D. M. Crump, "Truth," *DJG*, 859-862; Lester J. Kuyper, "Grace and Truth: An Old Testament Description of God, and Its Use in the Johannine Gospel," *Int* 18 (1964), 3-19; Ignace de la Potterie, "The Truth in Saint John," in John Ashton, ed. and trans., *The Interpretation of John* (IRT 9; 2d ed.; Philadelphia/London: Fortress/SPCK, 1986), 67-82; David J. Hawkin, "The Johannine Concept of Truth," *EQ* 59 (1987), 3-13; Anthony C. Thiselton, "Truth," *NIDNTT*, 3:874-902, esp. 879-880, 889-894; Jean Giblet, "Aspects of the Truth in the New Testament," in *Truth and Certainty* (ed. Edward Schillebeeckx and Bas van Iersel; New York: Herder & Herder, 1973), 35-42; and Geerhardus Vos, "'True' and 'Truth' in the Johannine Writings," *Biblical Review* 12 (1927), 507-520. See also James Barr, *The Semantics of Biblical Language* (London: SCM, 1961), 187-205; Roger Nicole, "The Biblical Concept of Truth," in *Scripture and Truth* (ed. D. A. Carson and John D. Woodbridge; Grand Rapids: Baker, 1992), 287-298; and L. Russ Bush III, "Knowing the Truth," *Faith & Mission* 11/2 (Spring 1994), 3-13.

11. On the charge of blasphemy against Jesus and a defense of its historicity, see especially Darrell L. Bock, *Blasphemy and Exaltation in Judaism: The Charge Against Jesus in Mark 14:53-65* (Grand Rapids: Baker, 2000 [1998]).

12. Cf., e.g., Thomas Söding, "Die Macht der Wahrheit und das Reich der Freiheit: Zur johanneischen Deutung des Pilatus-Prozesses (Joh 18, 28-19, 16," *ZTK* 93 (1996), 48-49.

13. This belief is also reflected in later Jewish writings, such as y. Sanh. 18a: "The seal of God is truth. What is truth? that he is the living God and the King eternal" (Beasley-Murray, *John*, 332, citing Adolf Schlatter, *Der Evangelist Johannes: Wie er spricht, denkt und glaubt* [2d ed.; Stuttgart: Calwer, 1948], 341; cf. B. F. Westcott, *The Gospel According to St. John* [orig. ed. 1881; repr. Grand Rapids: Eerdmans, 1975], 261, with reference to Lightfoot).

14. Cf. Beasley-Murray, *John*, 331: "Jesus is not speaking of truth in an abstract, or even general way, but specifically in relation to his ministry." Moreover, as C. K. Barrett, *The Gospel According to St. John* (2d ed., Philadelphia: Westminster, 1978), 538, notes, in John, truth is "truth in motion," entering and addressing the world, and liberating those who are capable of hearing it (8:32). Its ultimate point of reference is not a world of timeless forms but God's plan of salvation. Leon Morris, *The Gospel According to John* (NICNT; rev. ed.; Grand Rapids: Eerdmans, 1995), 260, notes the association of truth with God (and Jesus' ministry in fulfillment of God's covenant promises) in Paul's letter to the Romans (1:25; 3:7; 15:8).

15. Strauss and Baur are cited in Heinrich August Wilhelm Meyer, *Critical and Exegetical Handbook to the Gospel of John* (trans. William Urwick; New York/London: Funk & Wagnalls, 1884), 496. See also Maurice Casey, *Is John's Gospel True?* (London/New York: Routledge, 1996), 186: "Here, history has been rewritten to put more blame on 'the Jews.' " See also ibid., 183: ". . . we must infer that the whole account has been rewritten"; and ibid., 187: "This is extensively rewritten history. . . ."

16. James D. G. Dunn, *Jesus Remembered* (Grand Rapids: Eerdmans, 2003), 776: "John imagines a debate between Jesus and Pilate, in which Pilate is impressed by Jesus' answers and repeatedly insists, 'I find no case against him' (John 18.38; 19.4, 6)." At least at this point, surely a better title for Dunn's book than *Jesus Remembered* would have been *Jesus Imagined*! Dunn goes on to say that "tensions" "leave the role of Pilate in Jesus' execution tantalisingly obscure" and states that the Gospels' portrait of Pilate is "biased in his favor." He concludes, "At the very least, however, the primary responsibility for Jesus' execution should be firmly pinned to Pilate's record, and the first hints of an anti-Jewish tendency in the Gospels on this point should be clearly recognized and disowned" (776-777). However, Dunn's conclusion is itself biased and does not rest on a fair and balanced weighing of the evidence for or against the historicity of the account. It is not in keeping with proper scholarly procedure to dismiss John's presentation as "imagined" by way of mere assertion without argument. In fact, as the discussion below demonstrates, a strong case can be made for the historicity of John's account.

17. Andrew T. Lincoln, "Reading John: The Fourth Gospel under Modern and Postmodern Interrogation," in *Reading the Gospels Today* (McMaster New Testament Studies; ed. Stanley E. Porter; Grand Rapids: Eerdmans, 2004), 132, dismissing Craig L. Blomberg's *The Historical Reliability of John's*

Gospel (Leicester: Apollos, 2001) as an exercise in "strained argumentation." See also Lincoln's assertion later in his essay that "truth . . . is not to be confused with the factual accuracy of each detail of the Gospel but is the message of its overall narrative" (147). While a thorough response to Lincoln's claim is beyond the scope of this paper, it may be noted that, to the contrary, Lincoln's own reasoning is implausible that a Gospel that by his own admission centers to such a large degree on the question of truth would compromise the truth by telling a story that the author himself knew does not correspond to events in Jesus' ministry. Lincoln's logic, too, that a narrative may be wrong in the details but right in its overall message is far from unassailable.

18. For positive assessments of John's historicity, see Herman N. Ridderbos, *The Gospel of John: A Theological Commentary* (Grand Rapids: Eerdmans, 1997), 587-588; and D. A. Carson, *The Gospel According to John* (PNTC; Grand Rapids: Eerdmans, 1991), 587, who suggests as possible Johannine sources Jesus after the resurrection, court attendants who later became believers, or possibly some public court records. To this may be added the possibility of eyewitness testimony (cf. 18:15-16; 19:26-27, 35). See also the verdict of Raymond E. Brown, *The Gospel According to John XIII-XXI* (AB 29A; New York: Doubleday, 1970), 861, who concludes that "John's account of the trial is the most consistent and intelligible we have"; and the similar assessment by Söding, "Die Macht der Wahrheit und das Reich der Freiheit," 37: "[John's] presentation is more plausible historically than the Markan and Matthean one" (though see the false dichotomy between history and theology on p. 38).

19. Contra Casey, *Is John's Gospel True?* 183, who asserts, without substantiation, "Nor is it probable that the Roman governor would come out of the praetorium merely because Jewish authorities both wanted to see him, and declared him and his house unclean." Why is this so implausible? As discussed below, historical records suggest that Pilate's position had become increasingly vulnerable, so there is no reason why he would not have come out to the Jews to hear the charges they presented against Jesus. On a different note, the fact that Pilate condemned Jesus to be crucified on the basis of the charges made by "men of the highest standing among us" is confirmed by Josephus, Ant. 18.64 (cited in Dunn, *Jesus Remembered*, 776, n. 71).

20. *Sy ei ho basileus tōn Ioudaiōn*; Matt 27:11; Mark 15:2; Luke 23:3; John 18:33.

21. *Sy legeis*; Matt. 27:11; Mark 15:2; Luke 23:3; John 18:37. Ernst Bammel, "The Trial before Pilate," in *Jesus and the Politics of His Day* (ed. Ernst Bammel and C. F. D. Moule; Cambridge: Cambridge University Press, 1984), 417-419.

22. See further the discussion below.

23. Compare and contrast Carson, *John*, 571-572, who thinks John knew one or two of the Synoptics; and Brown, *Gospel According to John XIII-XI*, 787-791, who believes John wrote independently of the Synoptics.

24. Though see John 3:3, 5; 12:13-15. For a discussion of the relationship between the reference to the kingdom of God in Jesus' conversation with Nicodemus and Jesus' reference to his kingdom vis-à-vis Pilate see Martin Hengel, "Reich Christi, Reich Gottes und Weltreich im 4. Evangelium," *TBei* 14 (1983), 201-216; also in Martin Hengel and Anna Maria Schwemer, eds., *Königsherrschaft Gottes und himmlischer Kult im Judentum, Urchristentum und in der hellenistischen Welt* (WUNT 55; Tübingen: Mohr-Siebeck, 1991), 163-184. On the kingdom of God in Jesus' teaching, see Bock, *Jesus According to Scripture*, 565-593; Dunn, *Jesus Remembered*, 383-487. For the use of "kingdom of God" language in Second Temple literature, including the Dead Sea scrolls, see Dunn, *Jesus Remembered*, 385-386, n. 13, with further bibliographic references.

25. "Pontius" appears in the NT only in Luke 3:1, Acts 4:27, and 1 Tim. 6:13.

26. The Synoptists use the generic title "governor" (*hēgemōn*) with regard to Pilate (Matt. 27:2, 11, etc.; Luke 20:20). Tacitus, the Roman historian, calls him procurator (*Annals,* 15.44); Josephus uses the equivalent expression *epitropos* (J.W., 2.169). The famous Latin "Pilate inscription," found in Caesarea in 1961, identifies him as "prefect" (*praefectus*) of Judea: [PON]TIUS PILATUS [PRAEF]ECTUS IUDA[EA]E.

27. See Harold W. Hoehner, "Pontius Pilate," *DJG*, 615-617. For a treatment of Pilate in John's Gospel see Helen K. Bond, *Pontius Pilate in History and Interpretation* (SNTSMS 100; Cambridge: Cambridge University Press, 1998), 163-193.

28. Paul L. Maier, "Sejanus, Pilate, and the Date of the Crucifixion," *Church History* 37 (1968), 3-13.

29. Andreas J. Köstenberger, *John* (BECNT; Grand Rapids: Baker, 2004), 525, following Paul Maier, "Episode of the Golden Roman Shields at Jerusalem," *HTR* 62 (1969), 109-121; Hoehner, "Chronology," *DJG*, 121; idem, "Pontius Pilate," *DJG*, 616; idem, *Chronological Aspects of the Life of Christ* (Grand Rapids: Zondervan, 1977), 97-98, 105-111; idem, *Herod Antipas* (SNTSMS 17; Cambridge: Cambridge University Press, 1972), 172-183.

30. See also Philo, *Embassy to Gaius* 38, §302, where Pilate is shown to be concerned about excessive scrutiny by Caesar. I owe this reference to Bock, *Jesus According to Scripture*, 534, n. 62.

31. Cf. Hoehner, *Chronological Aspects*, 106, who says the event took place "[a]lmost immediately after his [Pilate's] arrival in Judea in A.D. 26." Hoehner dates the incident on December 2, A.D. 26.

32. This is dated by Hoehner, *Chronological Aspects*, 107, to "possibly the Passover of A.D. 32." Hoehner also notes that in A.D. 29/30 Pilate issued coins symbolizing Roman emperor worship but that after Sejanus's death in

the fall of A.D.31, emperor Tiberius instructed governors throughout the empire not to mistreat the Jews (Philo, *Leg.*, 159-161), with the result that, early in A.D. 32, Pilate stopped issuing these offensive coins (Hoehner, *Chronological Aspects*, 108-109).

33. As the Roman historian Suetonius documents, the emperor Tiberius could be a ruthless administrator (*Tiberius*, 58).

34. See, e.g., the collection of essays in Christopher Tuckett, ed., *The Messianic Secret* (IRT 1; Philadelphia/London: Fortress/SPCK, 1983).

35. Cf. Kevin J. Vanhoozer, *First Theology* (Downers Grove, IL: InterVarsity, 2002), chapters 9, 11; C. A. J. Coady, *Testimony: A Philosophical Study* (Oxford: Clarendon, 1994). I am grateful to Scott Swain for reminding me of this point.

36. In Jesus' coming, political dynamics are transcended by spiritual realities and history witnesses the clash of two kingdoms, the kingdom of God and the kingdom of darkness. Melba Maggay, "Jesus and Pilate: An Exposition of John 18:28-40," *Transformation* 8 (1991), 33.

37. Lincoln, "Reading John: The Fourth Gospel Under Modern and Postmodern Interrogation," 128, summarizing his thesis in *Truth on Trial: The Lawsuit Motif in the Fourth Gospel* (Peabody, MA: Hendrickson, 2000), on which see my review in *TrinJ* 22 (2001), 269-272.

38. See Köstenberger, *John*, 83-84.

39. As Bock, *Jesus According to Scripture*, 531, points out, the expression "king of the Jews" is used of Hasmonean kings in Josephus, *Ant.* 14.3.1 §36, and of Herod the Great in *Ant.* 16.10.2 §311. P. J. Tomson, "The Names Israel and Jew in Ancient Judaism and in the New Testament," *Bijdr* 47 (1986), 120-140, 266-289, followed by Dunn, *Jesus Remembered*, 262-265 (with further bibliographic references on 263, n. 32), argues that "Israel" is the term used by the Jews for themselves, while "Jews" is the expression used by others. This marks Pilate as an outsider.

40. Reimund Bieringer, "'My Kingship Is Not of This World' (John 18,36): The Kingship of Jesus and Politics," in *The Myriad Christ: Plurality and the Quest for Unity in Contemporary Christology* (ed. T. Merrigan and J. Haers; Leuven: Leuven University Press, 2000), 170: "Instead of giving a positive answer, Jesus says what his βασιλεία is not . . . in 18,36 there is no positive description of Jesus' kingship."

41. Edwyn C. Hoskyns, *The Fourth Gospel* (ed. and comp. Francis Noel Davey; 2d rev. ed.; London: Faber & Faber, 1947), 2:619. Beasley-Murray, *John*, 331, says that Jesus in what follows does declare what his kingdom is: "it is the Kingdom of Truth." But Jesus does not exactly say this; he first speaks about his kingdom, and then says he came to witness to the truth. What these two statements have in common is their avoidance of focusing on Jesus' kingship; but it may be best not to conflate Jesus' two pronouncements into the expression "kingdom of truth" but rather understand Jesus' claim that

he came to witness to the truth as an affirmation of the superiority of truth over the notion of kingdom, as a loftier dimension in which his kingdom shares but which is an even broader and more universal concept.

42. As mentioned, John's Gospel features forty-six uses of the *aleth-* word group compared to a combined total of ten for the Synoptics; the Johannine epistles contain twenty-seven further instances. What is more, as Rudolf Schnackenburg (*The Gospel According to St. John* [New York: Crossroad, 1990], 2:225) points out, "truth" in the Synoptic texts is largely without theological significance (cf. Matt. 22:16 = Mark 12:14 = Luke 20:21; Mark 5:33; 12:32; Luke 4:25; 22:59; the same is true for the Book of Acts: see 4:27; 10:34; 26:25). A fuller exploration of the semantic field of "truth" in John's Gospel would, apart from instances of the noun *alētheia*, also include an analysis of the related adjectives and adverbs *alēthēs*, *alēthinos*, and *alēthōs*, as well as other terms such as the double *amēn* (on which see the excursus in Swain, "Truth in the Gospel of John," 68-75; Crump, "Truth," *DJG*, 860; and Raymond E. Brown, *The Gospel According to John I-XII* [AB 29; New York: Doubleday, 1966], 499-501). However, for our present purposes it is sufficient to limit the scope of our study to the passages that feature the noun *alētheia*. For a brief history of the study of truth in John's Gospel in the twentieth century spanning the spectrum from Hellenism to a Jewish background see the Excursus: "The Johannine Concept of Truth," in Schnackenburg, *The Gospel According to St. John*, 2:225-226, discussing works by Büchsel (Hellenistic syncretism), Bultmann ("divine reality" in line with an existential interpretation of John's Gospel), Dodd (Hermetic literature), Becker (relationship between John and Qumran), and de la Potterie (Jewish background). Schnackenburg also provides a helpful survey of the Johannine usage and semantic categories as well as of the comparative and historical background (ibid., 2:227-237). See also the survey of recent scholarship on truth in the Gospel of John in Swain, "Truth in the Gospel of John," 4-10.

43. For a survey of the relevant instances of *alētheia* in John's Gospel see Morris, *Gospel According to John*, 260-262.

44. There are twenty-seven instances in the Hebrew Scriptures where the terms *ḥesed* and *'emeth* are juxtaposed, half of which are in the Psalms: Gen. 24:27, 49; 32:11; 47:29; Exod. 34:6; Josh. 2:12, 14; 2 Sam. 2:6; 15:20; Ps. 25:10; 40:11, 12; 57:4, 11; 61:8; 69:14; 85:11; 86:15; 89:15; 115:1; 117:2; 138:2; Prov. 3:3; 14:22; 16:6; 20:28.

45. Cf. Lindsay, "Truth in John," 131-133, with reference to Adolf Schlatter, *Der Glaube im Neuen Testament* (6th ed.; Stuttgart: Calwer, 1982 = 1927), 552 (see also ibid., 145, n. 68). As George Ernest Wright notes, "the 'grace and truth' of Jesus Christ (John 1.14) are not abstract virtues but the active *ḥesed* and *'emeth*, rooted in the covenant conception" (*God Who Acts: Biblical Theology as Recital* [London: SCM, 1954], 114, cited in Morris,

Gospel According to John, 261, n. 126; similarly, Schnackenburg, *Gospel According to St. John*, 1.272-273; 2.228).

46. See further the comments on 18:36-38 in this section below.

47. So Lindsay, "Truth in John," 135-137, with reference to Otto Betz, "'To Worship God in Spirit and in Truth': Reflections on John 4,20-26," in *Standing Before God. Studies on Prayer in Scriptures and in Tradition. In Honor of John M. Oesterreicher* (trans. Nora Quigley; New York: KTAV, 1981), 58-61, who also cites Qumran parallels. C. H. Dodd, *The Interpretation of the Fourth Gospel* (Cambridge: Cambridge University Press, 1953), 174-175, adduces Ps. 145:18 as a potential parallel.

48. The close verbal parallel between the Baptist and Jesus "bearing witness to the truth" in 5:33 and 18:37 (noted, e.g., by Brown, *Gospel According to John XIII-XXI*) follows a pattern linking Jesus' mission with that of selected followers such as Peter (12:33; 18:32; 21:19) and the disciple Jesus loved (1:18; 13:23; 21:20). See Köstenberger, *John*, 599. Raymond Brown, *Gospel According to John I-XII*, 224, cites the parallel wording in 1QS 8:6: "witnesses to the truth."

49. On the politically charged interchange between Jesus and "the Jews" in John 8, see Lincoln, "Reading John: The Fourth Gospel under Modern and Postmodern Interrogation," 138-143; and Stephen Motyer, *Your Father the Devil? A New Approach to John and 'the Jews'* (Carlisle: Paternoster, 1997).

50. See the discussion of John 8:30-47 in Lindsay, "Truth in John," 138-140.

51. Cf. Lincoln, "Reading John: The Fourth Gospel Under Modern and Postmodern Interrogation," 147-148, who notes that the "truth witnessed to by the Fourth Gospel involves the triune God," citing esp. 15:26.

52. Cf. Lindsay, "Truth in John," 140-141.

53. Cf. ibid., 140-143. Thiselton, "Truth," 892, notes that the Greek phrase in 17:17 is identical with the LXX form of Ps. 119:142 as found in Codex Sinaiticus (though not the MT and others LXX mss., which read "your law is truth"). The relevance of the references to truth in the farewell discourse for 18:33-38a is affirmed, among others, by Thomas L. Brodie, *The Gospel According to John: A Literary and Theological Commentary* (New York/Oxford: Oxford University Press, 1993), 534, who notes that in 17:17-19, as in 18:37-38a, there is a triple use of "truth." Brodie also alludes to the trinitarian dimension of truth in John's Gospel when he writes that for John, truth, "in practice," means "the revelation of the mystery of salvation in Jesus, the Son of the Father," and "the possibility of becoming Spirit-led children of God" (p. 535, citing de la Potterie).

54. Cf. 1 Tim. 6:13, which calls this Jesus' "good confession" before Pilate.

55. See John 3—4; 11:49-52; 12:20-50, esp. 12:32, 37-40; cf. Acts 1:8; 13:46-48; 28:17-31; Rom. 1:14-16. Note in this context the interesting suggestion made by Kuyper, "Grace and Truth," 14, that the reason why, of the phrase

"grace and truth" in 1:14 and 17, the word "truth" continues to be used while the word "grace" is not, is that the evangelist "intends to let the word truth carry the full import of the concept within the expression, grace and truth." In Pilate's case, of course, grace was available, but not effective owing to the governor's unbelief (18:37-38).

56. In another sense, while John "records no answer in words," Morris (*Gospel According to John*, 682) is surely correct that "the whole of the following narrative of the death and resurrection of Jesus is John's answer in action. On the cross and at the empty tomb we may learn what God's truth is." Morris makes the same point on pp. 260-261, where he also refers to Alf Corell, *Consummatum Est: Eschatology and Church in the Gospel of St. John* (London: SPCK, 1958), 161.

57. For a perceptive, albeit brief, study of the characterization of Jesus, Pilate, and the Jews in John 18:28—19:16a, plus a list of ironies in this unit, see Mark W. R. Stibbe, *John* (Sheffield: Sheffield Academic Press, 1993), 186-192. Stibbe notes that while Pilate evokes our sympathy, the Jewish leaders evoke the reader's antipathy. They are guilty of hypocrisy (18:28), choose Barabbas over Jesus (18:40), and, according to Stibbe, misquote a Passover hymn when they shout in 19:15, "We have no king but Caesar!" (p. 189).

58. See Andreas J. Köstenberger, "The Seventh Johannine Sign: A Study in John's Christology," *Bulletin of Biblical Research* 5 (1995), 87-103, where I provide an inferred Johannine definition of "sign" and argue against including Jesus' walking on the water in 6:16-21 and for including the temple clearing in 2:14-22 as a Johannine sign.

59. The word *houtos* ("this man") likely has a derogatory connotation.

60. Cf. Bock, *Jesus According to Scripture*, 535, n. 65, who also cites the Jewish national prayer, *Shemoneh Esreh*, benediction 11, which reads in an address to God, "May you be our King, you alone," and notes that "[a]t the Passover, the Jews would have affirmed the unique sovereignty of God" (*m. Ros Hassanah* 1.2).

61. At a higher level, of course, God uses the Jewish rejection of the Messiah to fulfill Scripture and to accomplish his salvation-historical purposes, but this is not to excuse the Jewish leaders' actions.

62. Cf. Bieringer, "My Kingship Is Not of This World," 171: "For a brief moment it seems as if Pilate was going to understand that Jesus claims a βασιλεία different from that of the Jews. But, as the inscription 'King of the Jews' which Pilate has put on the cross (19,19) demonstrates, Pilate ultimately remains closed to the religious dimension of Jesus' person and message."

63. Among the errors of judgments committed by Pilate (as listed by Stibbe, *John*, 188-189) are the following: he calls Jesus "the king of the Jews" (18:39), which further provokes the Jewish leaders; he ends up having to free Barabbas, which is hardly what Pilate had intended in the first place; he calls

Jesus "the man" (19:5), which may have unwelcome connotations to the ears of the Jews; and he finally brings Jesus out and says, "Behold your king!" (19:14). Most likely, these errors of judgment reveal Pilate's ignorance and ineptitude rather than constituting intentional provocations of the Jews.

64. The pronouns "you" (*hymeis*) and "your" (*hymōn*) in 18:31 are emphatic.

65. The fourth evangelist narrates Jesus' Roman trial in seven units, which display an oscillating pattern of outdoor and indoor scenes (18:29-32, 33-38a, 38b-40; 19:1-3, 4-7, 8-11, 12-15). R. Alan Culpepper, *The Anatomy of the Fourth Gospel* (Philadelphia: Fortress, 1983), 142, traces the identification of the seven scenes to R. H. Strachan, *The Fourth Gospel: Its Significance and Environment* (3d ed.; London, SCM, 1941), 310. Stibbe, *John*, 187, and Keener, *John*, 1:1097, propose a chiastic structure, with 19:1-3 in the center. Pilate's question, "What is truth?" in 18:38a is part of the second scene of the Johannine account of Jesus' Roman trial.

66. See the discussion of the Synoptic Gospels above.

67. Cf. Charles Homer Giblin, "John's Narration of the Hearing Before Pilate (John 18,28-19,16a," *Bib* 67 (1986), 227, n. 18; Bond, *Pontius Pilate*, 177. Hoehner, *Chronological Aspects*, 105, notes that Pilate's mentor Sejanus "was a dedicated anti-Semite who wanted to exterminate the Jewish race," citing Philo, *In Flaccum* 1; *Leg.*, 159-161.

68. Alfred Plummer, *The Gospel According to St. John* (orig. ed. 1882; Thornapple Commentaries; repr. Grand Rapids: Baker, 1981), 319, and Westcott, *Gospel According to St. John*, 261, detect impatience in Pilate's question in 18:38a, "What is truth?"

69. Commentators are widely agreed that Pilate's question was not sincere but rather flippant. William Barclay, *The Gospel of John* (rev. ed.; Philadelphia: Westminster, 1975), 2:242, and Leon Morris, *Gospel According to John*, 682, n. 91, quote Francis Bacon, who wrote in his essay *Of Truth*: "What is truth? said jesting Pilate; and would not stay for an answer," and suggests that Pilate asked the question "wistfully and wearily." Similarly, J. H. Bernard, *A Critical and Exegetical Commentary on the Gospel According to St. John* (ICC; Edinburgh: T. & T. Clark, 1928), 2:612: "perhaps wistful rather than cynical or careless." F. F. Bruce, *The Gospel of John* (Grand Rapids: Eerdmans, 1983), 354, speaks of a "curt dismissal" of the question by Pilate; John Calvin, *The Gospel According to St. John* (trans. T. H. L. Parker; Grand Rapids: Eerdmans, 1961), 2:168, characterizes Pilate's attitude as "disdainful" and believes the Roman governor spoke in "mockery," "anger," and "indignation," which he takes as evidence that Pilate was "forced to feel some inward pricking." Robert W. Yarbrough, *John* (Everyman's Bible Commentary; Chicago: Moody, 1991), 185, likewise finds Pilate's dismissal of Jesus' question "at least skeptical and perhaps sneering." By contrast, Hoskyns, *The Fourth Gospel*, 2:619-620, believes that "Pilate is neither indifferent nor sceptical, but simply incapable

of apprehending." Similarly, Colin G. Kruse, *John* (TNTC; Leicester: InterVarsity, 2003), 360, says that "Pilate was reduced to confusion." Plummer, *Gospel According to St. John*, 319, speaks of "the half-pitying, half-impatient, question of a practical man of the world, whose experience of life has convinced him that truth is a dream of enthusiasts." Westcott, *Gospel According to St. John*, 261, too, detects a hint of impatience in Pilate's question. But see cautions registered by Rudolf Bultmann (*Gospel of John* [trans. George R. Beasley-Murray; Oxford: Basil Blackwell, 1971], 656), who says the "question should not be psychologically interpreted"; echoed by Haenchen, *Gospel of John*, 2:180; idem, "Historie und Geschichte in den johanneischen Passionsberichten," in *Die Bibel und wir: Gesammelte Aufsätze* (Tübingen: Mohr-Siebeck, 1968), 2:196-198.

70. Cf. Bultmann, *Gospel of John*, 656. Note that both references to truth in Jesus' statement are articular: "to bear witness to the truth" and "everyone who is of the truth" (18:37) and that Pilate in his question shifts from articular and definite to anarthrous and unspecific: "What is truth?" (cf. J. Carl Laney, *John* [Moody Gospel Commentary; Chicago: Moody, 1992], 332: "Pilate did not ask what is the truth"; similarly, Plummer, *Gospel According to St. John*, 319).

71. While ostensibly asking about truth, Pilate in fact sought to avoid it. Heinrich Schlier, "Jesus und Pilatus nach dem Johannesevangelium," in *Die Zeit der Kirche* (Freiburg: Herder, 1958), 65.

72. Friedrich Nietzsche, *Twilight of the Idols and the Anti-Christ* (trans. R. J. Hollingdale; London: Penguin, 1990), 174, even credited Pilate with enriching the NT "with the only expression which possesses value—which is its criticism, its annihilation even: 'What is truth?'" (cited in Miroslav Volf, *Exclusion and Embrace: A Theological Exploration of Identity, Otherness, and Reconciliation* (Nashville: Abingdon, 1996), 270). For Nietzsche, disregard for truth went hand in hand with disregard for human (especially Jewish) life, as when he attributes to Pilate the thought, "One Jew more or less [i.e., Jesus]—what does it matter?" (*Twilight*, 174, cited in Volf, *Exclusion and Embrace*, 271). For Nietzsche, any belief in truth enslaves; only when one jettisons the very notion of truth is one truly free (*The Birth of Tragedy and The Genealogy of Morals* [trans. Francis Golffing; Garden City: Doubleday, 1956], 287, cited in Volf, *Exclusion and Embrace*, 270).

73. Culpepper, *Anatomy of the Fourth Gospel*, 143; cf. R. H. Lightfoot, *St. John's Gospel: A Commentary* (London: Oxford University Press, 1956), 311, who states that "the position now reached . . . is that he will take the side neither of accusers [18³⁵] nor of Accused [18³⁸], and that he seeks, as before, to avoid the responsibility of a decision." The parallel to Nicodemus is also adduced by Barrett, *Gospel According to St. John*, 538, who writes (citing Haenchen) that, "like Nicodemus (7.50f.), Pilate for all his fair play and open-mindedness is not of the truth; he is of this world." For an

assessment of Nicodemus as a character in John's Gospel see also Köstenberger, *John*, 117-120.

74. Cf., e.g., Bond, *Pontius Pilate*, 178, who notes that Pilate understands neither the nature of Jesus' kingship nor his reference to truth. Bond also notes that, in a sense, Pilate shows that he is "a Jew" (cf. 18:35) in that he joins the unbelieving world—epitomized by the Jewish leaders—in their rejection of Jesus (ibid., 179).

75. Cf. Thiselton, "Truth," 893, who points out that "Pilate remains baffled because there are certain questions about truth which can be answered only when a man is fully open to hear the witness of Jesus. This brings us back to the claim of Jn. 14:6, that Jesus Christ not only states the truth; he is the truth."

76. I am grateful to Scott Swain for helping me draw out this implication.

77. Bultmann, *Gospel of John*, 656.

78. Ibid., 657. For a critique of Bultmann's interpretation of Pilate as a representative of the state, see Giblin, "John's Narration of the Hearing Before Pilate," 226-227, with further bibliographic references on 226, n. 16. Giblin notes that, unlike Matthew and Luke, John never refers to Pilate as governor.

79. This is the first reference to Jesus as "the king of the Jews" in this Gospel (cf. 18:39; 19:3; 19:19, 21 [*bis*]; see also 18:37 [*bis*]; 19:12, 14, 15 [*bis*]). Earlier, Jesus had eluded efforts by the people to make him their king (6:15). Jesus is acknowledged as the "king of Israel" by Nathanael in 1:49 and hailed as such at the triumphal entry (12:13, 15, with reference to the messianic passages Ps. 118:25-26 [though "king of Israel" is the evangelist's epexegetical addition] and Zech. 9:9).

80. Bock, *Jesus According to Scripture*, 531.

81. The intense personal nature of the interchange and Jesus' standing his ground before Pilate is revealed in that both in 18:33, 34 and in 18:37, Jesus reciprocates to an emphatic "you" (*sy*) by Pilate with an emphatic "you" of his own: Pilate: "Are *you* the king of the Jews?" Jesus: "Do *you* say this of your own accord . . . ?" (18:33, 34); Pilate: "So you are a king?" Jesus: "*You* say that I am a king" (18:37; note also the personal pronoun in Pilate's question in 18:35: *egō* . . . *eimi*).

82. Bultmann, *Gospel of John*, 654; Brown, *Gospel According to John XIII-XXI*, 868; cited in Beasley-Murray, *John*, 330; Bieringer, "My Kingship Is Not of This World," 170.

83. See also Amos 9:11-12 (cited by James in Acts 15:16-18). Acts 1:3 records that Jesus spoke to his followers about the kingdom of God at some length prior to his ascension. Yet they still did not understand the time frame and progression involved in the establishment of Jesus' kingdom and hence asked him, "Lord, will you at this time restore the kingdom to Israel?" (Acts 1:6).

In Acts 3:20-21, Peter speaks about a future time of "refreshing" and restoration.

84. In the book of Revelation, the loud voices raised in heaven anticipate the consummation of this development: "The kingdom of the world has become the kingdom of our Lord and of his Christ, and he shall reign forever and ever" (11:15). Bieringer, "My Kingship Is Not of This World," 171, sees a parallel between the reference to God's kingdom presupposing a birth "from above" in 3:3, 5 and Jesus' kingdom being "not of this world" in 18:36.

85. As Beasley-Murray, *John*, 331, rightly notes, the fact that Jesus' kingdom is not of this world does not imply that it is "not *active* in this world," nor that it "*has nothing to do with this world*" (italics his). Jesus' kingdom affects this world, but it does not belong to it (Brown, *Gospel According to John XIII-XXI*, 869; Bultmann, *Gospel of John*, 657, both cited in Beasley-Murray, *John*, 331). Maggay, "Jesus and Pilate," 31, makes the important point that "while, on the one hand, it is wrong to politicize Jesus' Kingship . . . it is also just as inappropriate to spiritualize Jesus' Kingship and see it as entirely future." He refers to Mary's Magnificat, which makes clear that "the coming of the King and of his kingdom will mean a concrete historical reversal: the mighty will be overthrown and the humble and lowly lifted up." Hence the power of God becomes visible in the political struggles of our time.

86. This is in keeping with the Johannine motif of the "elusive Christ" (the term is Stibbe's: see Mark W. G. Stibbe, "The Elusive Christ: A New Reading of the Fourth Gospel," *JSNT* 44 [1991], 20-39, alluded to also in Stibbe, *John*, 187) and is an instance of what A. D. Nuttall calls "discontinuous dialogue," which is caused by Jesus' "technique of deliberate transcendence," creates suspense, and ironically contributes to his own condemnation (see A. D. Nuttall, *Overheard by God: Fiction and Prayer in Herbert, Milton, Dante and St John* [London: Methuen, 1980], 129, cited in Stibbe, *John*, 188).

87. Commentators (e.g., Bernard, *Gospel According to St. John*, 611; Meyer, *Gospel of John*, 494) regularly note the incredulous if not contemptuous nature of Pilate's question, "So you are a king?" in 18:37, which is underscored by the fact that the personal pronoun "you" (*sy*) is put last in the sentence.

88. Note the three references to "my kingdom" in 18:36, which forms an inclusion and contrasts with the two references to "God's kingdom" in 3:3, 5.

89. Though not quite in the way in which Bultmann, "ἀλήθεια," 246, conceives of it. Bultmann is at his existential best when he writes that 18:37 "shows again that ἀλήθεια is the self-revealing divine reality, and that its comprehension is not a free act of existence, but is grounded in the determination of existence by divine reality." More apropos is the remark by Westcott, *Gospel According to St. John*, 261: "Truth, absolute reality, is the realm of Christ. He marks out its boundaries; and every one who has a vital connexion with the Truth recognises His sway."

90. See especially. the echoes of Ezekiel 34 and other OT messianic passages in John 10, on which see Andreas J. Köstenberger, "Jesus the Good Shepherd Who Will Also Bring Other Sheep (John 10:16): The Old Testament Background of a Familiar Metaphor," *BBR* 12 (2002), 67-96. See also the discussion of the nature of Jesus' kingship in the context of his appearance before Pilate in Bond, *Pontius Pilate*, 169-171.

91. Kruse, *John*, 360.

92. As Ulrich Wilckens, *Das Evangelium nach Johannes* (NTD 4; Göttingen: Vandenhoeck & Ruprecht, 1998), 282, writes, Pilate "wants to remain judge rather than becoming a disciple" (*Er will Richter bleiben, nicht Jünger werden*).

93. Cf. Barclay, *John*, 2:43, who notes that Pilate had "not the courage to defy the world in spite of his past, and to take his stand with Christ and a future which was glorious." See also Beasley-Murray, *John*, 332, who notes that Jesus' statement "implicitly conveys an invitation," placing "Pilate in a situation of decision": "Jesus the prisoner sets his judge in the dock!"

94. As Bock, *Jesus According to Scripture*, 533, notes, Jesus had already said that his kingdom was not of this world and that he had "come into this world" (18:36-37).

95. In 16:28 Jesus had told the Eleven, "I came from the Father and have come into the world, and now I am leaving the world and going to the Father." In 12:46, Jesus had said, "I have come into the world as light, so that whoever believes in me may not remain in darkness."

96. Cf. the Jewish leaders' self-reference as having "handed over" (*paredōkamen*) Jesus to Pilate in 18:30 and Pilate's reference to Jesus' "own nation and the chief priests" having "handed" him over (*paredōkan*) to him in 18:35. See also Jesus' comment that if his kingdom were of this world, his servant would fight to prevent his arrest by the Jewish leaders (18:36; so rightly the NIV, TNIV, and the NLT, though almost all other translations incorrectly render the phrase *paradothō tois Ioudaiois* "handed over to the Jews"; e.g., KJV; NKJV, NASB, NRSV, ESV, HCSB).

97. The term is Ridderbos's: Ridderbos, *Gospel of John*, 587.

98. See the historical survey above.

99. Cf. Keener, *John*, 2:1114, citing Paul D. Duke, *Irony in the Fourth Gospel* (Atlanta: John Knox, 1985), 130; Ben Witherington, *John's Wisdom: A Commentary on the Fourth Gospel* (Louisville: Westminster John Knox, 1995), 292.

100. Volf, *Exclusion and Embrace*, 266. Volf 's entire discussion of Jesus' trial before Pilate (entitled "Jesus Before Pilate: Truth Against Power") on 264-271 repays careful reading.

101. Cf. Lincoln, "Reading John: The Fourth Gospel Under Modern and Postmodern Interrogation," 145, who speaks of "crucifying the truth."

102. I am aware that calling Pilate a "comparatively minor" character in the Johannine trial narrative is potentially explosive and open to misrepresentation, but in the spirit of Luther, as an interpreter of the Johannine narrative, "Here I stand, I can do no other." On the alleged anti-Semitism of John's Gospel, see Reimund Bieringer, Didier Pollefeyt, and Frederique Vandecasteele-Vanneuville, eds., *Anti-Judaism and the Fourth Gospel* (Louisville: Westminster John Knox, 2001) and the fuller volume with the same title published by Royal Van Gorcum in 2001. But see my review of this work in *Themelios* 28/2 (2003), 71-73.

103. Cf. Rodney A. Whitacre, *John* (IVPNTC; Downers Grove, IL: InterVarsity, 1999), 443: "So now both Jew and Gentile have been given a chance to respond to the one come from God."

104. The phrase is Volf's (*Exclusion and Embrace*, 266), to whose suggestive treatment on 264-271 this paragraph is partially indebted. See the previous references to Volf 's work above.

105. The phrase is Lincoln's ("Reading John: The Fourth Gospel Under Modern and Postmodern Interrogation," 145), to whose treatment on 143-146 this paragraph is partially indebted.

106. Cf. Lincoln, "Reading John: The Fourth Gospel Under Modern and Postmodern Interrogation," 143, who sums up postmodernism's own "grand narrative" as holding that "power produces what passes for truth and this truth then becomes the means by which the powerful wield more power." As Lincoln rightly points out, there is "a cost to leaving open the question of truth," because "[t]he person who treats the question about truth with contempt has no compelling reason not to treat human life with contempt." Lincoln aptly notes that "[w]e need to be alert not only to the dangers but also to the potential for human wellbeing bound up with claims to truth, including that of the Fourth Gospel, which sees truth embodied in Jesus" (ibid., 144).

107. I am indebted for the following story to Söding, "Die Macht der Wahrheit und das Reich der Freiheit," 57-58. See Václav Havel, "The Power of the Powerless" (trans. P. Wilson), in *Living in Truth: Twenty-two Essays Published on the Occasion of the Award of the Erasmus Prize to Václav Havel* (ed. Jan Vladislav; London/Boston: Faber and Faber, 1989 [1986]), 36-122 (dated October 1978). The original title of Havel's essay is *Versuch, in der Wahrheit zu leben: Von der Macht der Ohnmächtigen* (trans. Gabriel Laub; Reinbek bei Hamburg: Rowohlt, 1980). See also Václav Havel, "Ein Wort über das Wort. Rede aus Anlass der Verleihung des Friedenspreises des deutschen Buchhandels am 15. 10. 1989," in *Am Anfang war das Wort* (Reinbek bei Hamburg: Rowohlt, 1989), 207-224.

CHAPTER TWO: TRUTH AND CONTEMPORARY CULTURE

1. Jay A. Barnes, *A Pack of Lies: Toward a Sociology of Lying* (Cambridge: Cambridge University Press, 1994), 60.

2. George Steiner, *Grammars of Creation* (New Haven: Yale University Press, 2001), 161.

3. Louis Menand, *The Metaphysical Club* (New York: Farrar, Straus, and Giroux, 2001), x-xi.

4. Jean-François Lyotard, *The Postmodern Condition: A Report on Knowledge* (Theory and History of Literature 10; trans. Geoff Bennington and Brian Massumi; Minneapolis: University of Minnesota Press, 1984), xxiv.

5. Philip D. Kenneson, "There is No Such Thing as 'Objective Truth,' and It's a Good Thing, Too," in *Christian Apologetics in the Postmodern World* (ed. Timothy R. Phillips and Dennis L. Okholm; Downers Grove, IL: InterVarsity, 1995), 161.

6. Stanley J. Grenz, *Renewing the Center: Evangelical Theology in a Post-Theological Era* (Grand Rapids: Baker, 2000), 185.

7. Ibid., 101.

8. Stephen J. Wellum, "Postconservatism, Biblical Authority, and Recent Proposals for Re-Doing Evangelical Theology: A Critical Analysis," in *Reclaiming the Center: Confronting Evangelical Accommodation in Postmodern Times* (ed. Millard J. Erickson, Paul Kjöss Helseth, and Justin Taylor; Wheaton, IL: Crossway, 2004), 186.

9. Carl F. H. Henry, *God, Revelation, and Authority*, Vol. 1 (Waco, TX: Word, 1976), 215.

10. John G. Stackhouse, Jr., "Review of Gary J. Dorrien, The Remaking of Evangelical Theology," *Christian Century* (July 19, 2000), 767.

CHAPTER THREE: TRUTH, CONTEMPORARY PHILOSOPHY, AND THE POSTMODERN TURN

1. For a helpful introduction to postmodernism, see Joseph Natoli, *A Primer to Postmodernity* (Oxford: Blackwell, 1997). See also J. P. Moreland and William Lane Craig, *Philosophical Foundations for a Christian Worldview* (Downers Grove, IL: InterVarsity, 2003), Chapter 6; Garrett DeWeese and J. P. Moreland, "The Premature Report of Foundationalism's Demise," in *Reclaiming the Center: Evangelical Accommodation in a Post-Theological Era* (ed. Justin Taylor, Millard Erickson, and Paul Kjöss Helseth; Wheaton, IL: Crossway, 2005), 81-105.

2. Brian McLaren, "Emergent Evangelism," *Christianity Today* 48/11 (November 2004), 42-43.

3. Philip Kennison, "There's No Such Thing As Objective Truth, and It's a Good Thing, Too," in *Christian Apologetics in the Postmodern World* (ed.

Timothy Philips and Dennis Okholm; Downers Grove, IL: InterVarsity, 1995), 157.

4. Stanley Grenz, *Revisioning Evangelical Theology* (Downers Grove, IL: InterVarsity, 1993), 15.

5. Stanley J. Grenz and John R. Franke, *Beyond Foundationalism: Shaping Theology in a Postmodern Context* (Louisville: Westminster John Knox, 2001), 38. Grenz and Franke use the phrase "the demise of foundationalism" ten times in the first fifty-four pages (Part I) of the book.

6. Rodney Clapp, "How Firm a Foundation: Can Evangelicals Be Nonfoundationalists?" in *Border Crossings: Christian Trespasses on Popular Culture and Public Affairs* (Grand Rapids: Brazos, 2000), 19-32.

7. Nancey Murphy, *Anglo-American Postmodernity: Philosophical Perspectives on Science, Religion and Ethics* (Boulder, CO: Westview, 1997), 131-132.

8. Michael R. DePaul, "Preface," in *Resurrecting Old-Fashioned Foundationalism* (ed. Michael R. DePaul; Lanham, MD: Rowman and Littlefield, 2001), vii.

9. Natoli, *Primer*, 18.

10. Richard Rorty, *Contingency, Irony and Solidarity* (New York: Cambridge University Press, 1989), 4-5.

11. Grenz, *Revisioning Evangelical Theology*, 73-74.

12. Esther Lightcap Meek, *Longing to Know: The Philosophy of Knowledge for Ordinary People* (Grand Rapids: Brazos, 2003), 146-147.

13. Ibid., 148.

14. Ibid., 179.

15. Ibid., 182.

16. Ibid., 167. For the best, most accessible treatment of postmodernism available, see Douglas Groothuis, *Truth Decay* (Downers Grove, IL: InterVarsity, 2000).

17. I wish to thank Garry DeWeese for helpful comments on an earlier draft of this paper.

CHAPTER FOUR: LOST IN INTERPRETATION? TRUTH, SCRIPTURE, AND HERMENEUTICS

1. This is a revised version—the director's cut!—of the plenary paper I presented at the annual ETS meeting in San Antonio in November 2004. I want to thank Mark Bowald for his helpful comments on the original version. The revised version includes additional material that interacts with Carl Raschke's recent criticism of inerrancy (see below).

2. For further development of this theme, see Stanley J. Grenz, "Concerns of a Pietist with a Ph.D.," *Wesleyan Theological Journal* 37 (2002), 58-76.

3. Aidan Nichols, *Discovering Aquinas: An Introduction to His Life, Word, and Influence* (Grand Rapids: Eerdmans, 2002), 181.

4. Attempts at historical one-upmanship are similarly inconclusive. There are now on the market a number of genealogies each of which purports to demonstrate the ancient (or not) pedigree of the doctrine of inerrancy (see Thomas Buchan, "Inerrancy as Inheritance? Competing Genealogies of Biblical Authority," in Vincent Bacote, Laura C. Miguélez, and Dennis L. Okholm, eds., *Evangelicals & Scripture: Tradition, Authority, and Hermeneutics* [Downers Grove, IL: InterVarsity, 2004], 42-54). However, to believe that demonstrating historical provenance is equivalent to demonstrating a position's truth is to succumb to the genetic fallacy. One can neither prove nor disprove the truth of a position by showing where it came from.

5. I document both the death and the return of the author in my *Is There a Meaning in This Text? The Bible, the Reader, and the Morality of Literary Knowledge* (Grand Rapids: Zondervan, 1998).

6. See Iain Provan, V. Phillips Long, and Tremper Longman III, *A Biblical History of Israel* (Louisville: Westminster John Knox, 2003), 79-81.

7. Gianni Vattimo, *Beyond Interpretation: The Meaning of Hermeneutics for Philosophy* (Stanford, CA: Stanford University Press, 1997), 1.

8. Ibid., 5.

9. Vattimo himself notes the self-contradictory nature of this claim: if philosophical hermeneutics is the discovery of the "fact" that there are different perspectives on the world, then this would be a fact, not an interpretation, and would contradict the very point they are trying to make.

10. *For Self-Examination* (trans. Edna and Howard Hong; Minneapolis: Augsburg, 1940), 36.

11. Carl Raschke, *The Next Reformation: Why Evangelicals Must Embrace Postmodernity* (Grand Rapids: Baker, 2004).

12. Craig Detweiler and Barry Taylor, *A Matrix of Meanings: Finding God in Pop Culture* (Grand Rapids: Baker, 2003), 301.

13. Raschke, *The Next Reformation*, 119.

14. And on how it understands the nature and function of doctrine. Hence the purpose of the present essay: to reflect on the links between biblical interpretation and doctrinal truth. For a constructive proposal on the nature of doctrine, see my *The Drama of Doctrine: A Canonical-Linguistic Approach to Christian Theology* (Louisville: Westminster John Knox, 2005).

15. This description of Aquinas is similar to what George A. Lindbeck calls the "cognitive-propositionalist" type of theology (*The Nature of Doctrine: Religion and Theology in a Postliberal Age* [Philadelphia: Westminster, 1984]). Lindbeck identifies Aquinas with a "modest" cognitive-propositionalism (66).

16. Aidan Nichols, *Discovering Aquinas: An Introduction to His Life, Work, and Influence* (Grand Rapids: Eerdmans, 2002), 21. Though Aquinas speaks of theology as a *scientia* or "science," we would do well to recognize its peculiar nature: while doctrine involves a certain participation in God's cognition (e.g., thinking God's thoughts after him), such participation—faith—is a gift of grace. See John I. Jenkins, *Knowledge and Faith in Thomas Aquinas* (Cambridge: Cambridge University Press, 1997), esp. 66-77.

17. Thomas Aquinas, *Summa Theologiae* 1a, 1, 4. Aquinas distinguishes theology from other sciences by pointing out that its first principles are the articles of faith, not something derived from reason or observation.

18. Avery Dulles treats "conservative evangelicalism" as exhibit number one of the tendency to see revelation as doctrine (*Models of Revelation* [Garden City, NY: Doubleday, 1983], chap. 3).

19. Charles Hodge, *Systematic Theology*, 3 vols., 1:18.

20. Carl F. H. Henry, *God, Revelation and Authority*, Vol. III (Waco, TX: Word, 1979), 456. Note that Henry, unlike other evangelicals, conflates sentences and propositions. For a further development of this point, see my "The Semantics of Biblical Literature," in D. A. Carson and John D. Woodbridge, eds., *Hermeneutics, Authority, and Canon* (Grand Rapids: Baker, 1995), esp. 57-59.

21. Henry comes close to what literary critics call the "heresy of propositional paraphrase" when he suggests that the truth expressed in literary forms such as poetry and parable may be expressed in "declarative propositions" (*God, Revelation & Authority*, 3:463). Even speech acts such as promising and commanding can be "translated into propositions" (477). Such paraphrases and translations are necessary for Henry because "the primary concern of revelation is the communication of truth" (477).

22. *God, Revelation, and Authority*, I:238-239.

23. Dulles, *Models of Revelation*, 39.

24. See David Alan Williams, "Scripture, Truth and our Postmodern Context," in *Evangelicals & Scripture*, chap. 12.

25. Roger Nicole and others have demonstrated that the biblical concept of truth emphasizes reliability, not mirroring.

26. To enter into a genuine faith relation with God "we must set aside the dualism of subject and object that has overshadowed the tradition of Western thinking" (Raschke, *The Next Reformation*, 212).

27. So Ludwig Wittgenstein: "A proposition is a picture of reality" (*Tractatus Logico-Philosophicus* [London: Routledge & Kegan Paul, 1961], 4:01).

28. *To Know and Love God: Method for Theology* (Wheaton, IL: Crossway, 2003), 358.

29. Wittgenstein, *Tractatus*, 4:002.

30. There are other types of precision or clarity than the scientific. It has been

said, for example, that poetry is "the best words put in the best order." Similarly, because we are dealing with the Bible as God's word, we have good reason to believe that the biblical words are the right words in the right order, though as I shall argue below, we need to work hard to recognize the variety of literary orders that exist in Scripture. Part of the answer to emergentists like Raschke is to acknowledge that there are other orders in Scripture than the logical-propositional. Related to this is the further point that each of the Bible's literary forms may have its own "logic" or rationality—that is, its own way of making sense (and truth).

31. Henry, *God, Revelation, and Authority*, 4:175.

32. Harrisburg, PA: Trinity Press International, 1999.

33. Peter Enns, "Apostolic Hermeneutics and an Evangelical Doctrine of Scripture: Moving Beyond a Modernist Impasse," *WTJ* 65 (2003), 280.

34. Raschke, *The Next Reformation*, 122. For similar criticisms, see Henry H. Knight III, *A Future for Truth: Evangelical Theology in a Postmodern World* (Nashville: Abingdon, 1997), chap. 5: "The Inadequacies of Propositionalism"; Stanley J. Grenz, "Nurturing the Soul, Informing the Mind: The Genesis of the Evangelical Scripture Principle," in *Evangelicals & Scripture*, chap. 1; Nancey Murphy, *Beyond Liberalism and Fundamentalism: How Modern Philosophy Set the Theological Agenda* (Valley Forge, PA: Trinity Press International, 1996). Raschke blames the Princetonians for turning biblical authority into an epistemological principle. For a slightly different account, see William Abraham, *Canon and Criterion in Christian Theology* (Oxford: Clarendon, 1998).

35. One problem in moving to "statement" too fast is that one overlooks the nature and purpose of the particular authorial discourse. Strictly speaking, sentences do not refer; rather, authors use sentences to refer (or not). We shall return to the notion of authorial intention below.

36. Positivism is the quintessentially modern philosophical position that recognizes as facts observable phenomena only and strives for objective knowledge of the facts untainted by emotions, values, or faith.

37. So George Hunsinger, "What Can Evangelicals & Postliberals Learn from Each Other? The Carl Henry-Hans Frei Exchange Reconsidered," in Timothy R. Philips and Dennis L. Okholm, eds., *The Nature of Confession* (Downers Grove, IL: InterVarsity, 1996), 142.

38. Raschke, *The Next Reformation*, 131.

39. James Barr, *The Bible in the Modern World* (London: SCM, 1973), 125.

40. C. S. Lewis, "Myth Became Fact," in *God in the Dock: Essays on Theology and Ethics* (Grand Rapids: Eerdmans, 1970), 66.

41. I have a very flexible notion of "things." The things about which the Bible speaks do not all have to be empirically verifiable. Many of the things of which the prophets and apostles speak are eschatological: "already" actual

but "not yet" fully actual. Clearly, eschatological statements burst the old wineskins of modern positivist theories of language and reference.

42. G. A. Yee, "Introduction: Why Judges," in G. A. Yee, ed., *Judges and Method: New Approaches in Biblical Studies* (Minneapolis: Fortress, 1995), 11-12.

43. I develop these themes at much greater length in *The Drama of Doctrine*.

44. See Jo-Ann Brant, *Dialogue and Drama: Elements of Greek Tragedy in the Fourth Gospel* (Peabody, MA: Hendrickson, 2004).

45. The notion of "breathing space" comes from Hans W. Frei, "Conflicts in Interpretation: Resolution, Armistice, or Co-existence," in George Hunsinger and William C. Placher, eds., *Theology and Narrative: Selected Essays* (New York: Oxford University Press, 1993), 162.

46. The term comes from Enns, "Apostolic Hermeneutics," 277.

47. See Calvin, *A Harmony of the Gospels: Matthew, Mark, and Luke* in *Calvin's NT Commentaries* (trans. A. W. Morrison; ed. David W. Torrance and Thomas F. Torrance; Grand Rapids: Eerdmans, 1975]), 1:155.

48. Provan, *Biblical History*, 81.

49. Ibid.

50. See Mary E. Healy, "Behind, in Front of . . . or Through the Text? The Christological Analogy and the Lost World of Biblical Truth," in Craig Bartholomew et al., eds., *"Behind the Text": History and Biblical Interpretation* (Grand Rapids: Zondervan, 2003), 186.

51. Henry, *God, Revelation, and Authority*, 4:176.

52. See the discussion in Kent Sparks, "The Sun Also Rises: Accommodation in Inscripturation and Interpretation," in *Evangelicals & Scripture*, 112-132.

53. Note that the very fact that Scripture is written in Hebrew and Greek is already a kind of accommodation.

54. So Sparks, "The Sun Also Rises," 128-131.

55. Henry, *God, Revelation, and Authority*, 4:181.

56. Ibid., 205 (emphasis mine).

57. Henry also appeals to authorial meaning as the only norm of valid interpretation, the sole antidote to what he terms "hermeneutical nihilism" (*God, Revelation, and Authority*, Vol. 4, chap. 13).

58. By "postconservative" I understand an approach that, while recognizing the propositional component of speech acts, does not reduce language to reference or the cognitive dimension of theology to propositional statements. A postconservative theology affirms a plurality of normative points of view in Scripture, each of which is authoritative because each discloses a particular aspect of the truth.

59. I learned this valuable lesson from my former theology teacher, John Frame.

See Frame, *The Doctrine of the Knowledge of God* (Grand Rapids: Baker, 1987), 221.

60. See Marcus Borg, *Reading the Bible Again for the First Time: Taking the Bible Seriously but Not Literally* (San Francisco: HarperCollins, 2002).

61. Martha Nussbaum, *Love's Knowledge: Essays on Philosophy and Literature* (New York: Oxford University Press, 1990), 3.

62. Raschke, *The Next Reformation*, 119.

63. Ibid., 143.

64. Cited in Martin Chemnitz, *Examination of Council of Trent, Part 1* (trans. Fred Kramer; St. Louis: Concordia, 1971), 307.

65. Calvin, "Prefatory Address," section 5, *Institutes*.

66. *Truth on Trial: The Lawsuit Motif in the Fourth Gospel* (Peabody, MA: Hendrickson, 2000), 476.

67. See David L. Jeffrey and Anthony C. Thiselton, "Hermeneutics," in David Lyle Jeffrey, ed., *A Dictionary of Biblical Tradition in English Literature* (Grand Rapids: Eerdmans, 1992), 347-349.

68. For a more considered response to postmodernity, see my "Pilgrim's Digress: Christian Thinking on and About the Post/modern Way," in Myron Penner, ed., *Christianity and the Postmodern Turn* (Grand Rapids: Brazos, 2005).

69. Brian Davies, *The Thought of Thomas Aquinas* (Oxford: Clarendon, 1992), 277.

70. See Williams, "Scripture, Truth and our Postmodern Context," 240-241 for the fittingness of the "walking the way" metaphor for Christian truth.

EPILOGUE

1. David R. Liefeld, "God's Word or Male Words? Postmodern Conspiracy Culture and Feminist Myths of Christian Origins," *JETS* 48/3 (2005), 449-473.

2. Adolf Schlatter, *Do We Know Jesus? Daily Insights for the Mind and Soul* (Grand Rapids: Kregel, 2005), 19.

3. For fuller expressions of Vanhoozer's multifaceted proposals see also his following works: *Is There a Meaning in This Text? The Bible, The Reader, and the Morality of Literary Knowledge* (Grand Rapids: Zondervan, 1998); *First Theology: God, Scripture & Hermeneutics* (Downers Grove, IL: InterVarsity, 2002); and *The Drama of Doctrine: A Canonical-Linguistic Approach to Christian Theology* (Louisville: Westminster John Knox, 2005).

SCRIPTURE INDEX